D0881200

DATE DUE

Gangs

Other Books in the Social Issues Firsthand Series:

SOCIAL ISSUES
FIRSTHAND

Gangs

Laurie Willis, Book Editor

GREENHAVEN PRESS
A part of Gale, Cengage Learning

GALE
CENGAGE Learning™

Detroit • New York • San Francisco • New Haven, Conn • Waterville, Maine • London

Christine Nasso, *Publisher*
Elizabeth Des Chenes, *Managing Editor*

© 2009 Greenhaven Press, a part of Gale, Cengage Learning.

Gale and Greenhaven Press are registered trademarks used herein under license.

For more information, contact:
Greenhaven Press
27500 Drake Rd.
Farmington Hills, MI 48331-3535
Or you can visit our Internet site at gale.cengage.com

For product information and technology assistance, contact us at

Gale Customer Support, 1-800-877-4253
For permission to use material from this text or product, submit all requests online at
www.cengage.com/permissions

Further permissions questions can be emailed to permissionrequest@cengage.com

Articles in Greenhaven Press anthologies are often edited for length to meet page require-ments. In addition, original titles of these works are changed to clearly present the main thesis and to explicitly indicate the author's opinion. Every effort is made to ensure that Greenhaven Press accurately reflects the original intent of the authors. Every effort has been made to trace the owners of copyrighted material.

Cover image copyright Joshua Haviv, 2008. Used under license from Shutterstock.com.

LIBRARY OF CONGRESS CATALOGING-IN-PUBLICATION DATA

Gangs / Laurie Willis, book editor.
   p. cm. -- (Social issues firsthand)
   Includes bibliographical references and index.
   ISBN 978-0-7377-4253-4 (hardcover)
   1. Gangs--United States--Juvenile literature. 2. Gangs--Juvenile literature.
   I. Willis, Laurie.
   HV6439.U5G3583 2008
   364.106'60973--dc22
                                                      2008029733

Printed in the United States of America
2 3 4 5 6 7 12 11 10 09

Contents

Chapter 2: The Impact of Gang-Related Violence

Chapter 3: Working to Curtail Gang Activity

Foreword

Social issues are often viewed in abstract terms. Pressing challenges such as poverty, homelessness, and addiction are viewed as problems to be defined and solved. Politicians, social scientists, and other experts engage in debates about the extent of the problems, their causes, and how best to remedy them. Often overlooked in these discussions is the human dimension of the issue. Behind every policy debate over poverty, homelessness, and substance abuse, for example, are real people struggling to make ends meet, to survive life on the streets, and to overcome addiction to drugs and alcohol. Their stories are ubiquitous and compelling. They are the stories of everyday people—perhaps your own family members or friends—and yet they rarely influence the debates taking place in state capitols, the national Congress, or the courts.

The disparity between the public debate and private experience of social issues is well illustrated by looking at the topic of poverty. Each year the U.S. Census Bureau establishes a poverty threshold. A household with an income below the threshold is defined as poor, while a household with an income above the threshold is considered able to live on a basic subsistence level. For example, in 2003 a family of two was considered poor if its income was less than $12,015; a family of four was defined as poor if its income was less than $18,810. Based on this system, the bureau estimates that 35.9 million Americans (12.5 percent of the population) lived below the poverty line in 2003, including 12.9 million children below the age of eighteen.

Commentators disagree about what these statistics mean. Social activists insist that the huge number of officially poor Americans translates into human suffering. Even many families that have incomes above the threshold, they maintain, are likely to be struggling to get by. Other commentators insist that the statistics exaggerate the problem of poverty in the United States. Compared to people in developing countries, they point out, most so-called poor families have a high quality of life. As stated by journalist Fidelis Iyebote, "Cars are owned by 70 percent of 'poor' households. . . . Color televisions belong to 97 percent of the 'poor' [and] videocassette recorders belong to nearly 75 percent. . . . Sixty-four percent have microwave ovens, half own a stereo system, and over a quarter possess an automatic dishwasher."

However, this debate over the poverty threshold and what it means is likely irrelevant to a person living in poverty. Simply put, poor people do not need the government to tell them whether they are poor. They can see it in the stack of bills they cannot pay. They are aware of it when they are forced to choose between paying rent or buying food for their children. They become painfully conscious of it when they lose their homes and are forced to live in their cars or on the streets. Indeed, the written stories of poor people define the meaning of poverty more vividly than a government bureaucracy could ever hope to. Narratives composed by the poor describe losing jobs due to injury or mental illness, depict horrific tales of childhood abuse and spousal violence, recount the loss of friends and family members. They evoke the slipping away of social supports and government assistance, the descent into substance abuse and addiction, the harsh realities of life on the streets. These are the perspectives on poverty that are too often omitted from discussions over the extent of the problem and how to solve it.

Greenhaven Press's *Social Issues Firsthand* series provides a forum for the often-overlooked human perspectives on society's most divisive topics of debate. Each volume focuses on one social issue and presents a collection of ten to sixteen narratives by those who have had personal involvement with the topic. Extra care has been taken to include a diverse range of perspectives. For example, in the volume on adoption, readers will find the stories of birth parents who have made an adoption plan, adoptive parents, and adoptees themselves. After exposure to these varied points of view, the reader will have a clearer understanding that adoption is an intense, emotional experience full of joyous highs and painful lows for all concerned.

The debate surrounding embryonic stem cell research illustrates the moral and ethical pressure that the public brings to bear on the scientific community. However, while nonexperts often criticize scientists for not considering the potential negative impact of their work, ironically the public's reaction against such discoveries can produce harmful results as well. For example, although the outcry against embryonic stem cell research in the United States has resulted in fewer embryos being destroyed, those with Parkinson's, such as actor Michael J. Fox, have argued that prohibiting the development of new stem cell lines ultimately will prevent a timely cure for the disease that is killing Fox and thousands of others.

Each book in the series contains several features that enhance its usefulness, including an in-depth introduction, an annotated table of contents, bibliographies for further research, a list of organizations to contact, and a thorough index. These elements—combined with the poignant voices of people touched by tragedy and triumph—make the Social Issues Firsthand series a valuable resource for research on today's topics of political discussion.

Introduction

The U.S. Department of Justice, in its report *National Youth Gang Survey Trends from 1996 to 2000*, states that one hundred percent of cities with a population of over 250,000 reported persistent gang activity. Smaller cities and many rural areas also reported a significant gang presence. When considering the spread of gangs, one of the key questions that arises is: What motivates young people to join gangs?

There are a number of studies that list the factors in families and society that contribute to the prevalence of "at risk" youth, those young people who are less likely to succeed in school, often drop out, and frequently become involved in gangs, crime, and delinquency. According to a 1994 report by the United States Office of Juvenile Justice and Delinquency Prevention, "Reasons for joining gangs include a need or wish for recognition, status, safety or security, power, excitement, and new experience." The study goes on to explain that in some socially deprived areas, gangs are considered a normal and respectable extension of the family system.

Being a member of a gang provides a sense of belonging, an "instant family." For some, the gang replaces what their family of origin does not provide. For others, gangs are a way of life, even within their own family. Parents, uncles, or older siblings already belong. In some neighborhoods, most of the young people are gang members as a matter of course.

Abraham Maslow's hierarchy of human needs states that after the basic physical needs—food, water, oxygen—are met, the next most important needs are for safety, a sense of affection and belonging, and a sense of esteem and respect. Maslow's list and the list of reasons for joining gangs are very similar. The fact that normal, healthy human needs are not being met in their home and family life is a significant factor that leads many young people to join gangs.

In neighborhoods where gang violence is prevalent, belonging to a gang feels like the safer option for many. A new member feels that he or she will be protected from other gangs. That sense of protectedness, however, is illusory. At one time, gang violence usually took the form of fist fights, and gang members actually could protect one another from violence. Currently, however, guns are used as often as fists, and protection from bullets is hard to come by. The response to intergang gun violence usually takes the form of retaliation, which then provokes a desire for revenge by the other side, and the violence escalates to the point where no gang member is safe. In addition, even the act of being initiated into a gang is often a violent ritual. Called by a variety of names, including "jumping in" or "courting in," the process usually requires the new member to fight several gang members for a specified length of time before being accepted as a member.

Another reason often given for joining a gang is the sense of status and recognition felt by members, fulfilling the need for self-esteem and respect. As a member of a gang, a person may feel that he or she is superior to those not in the gang. Members often take on a gang name, wear gang colors, and occupy a particular place in the community. Increased respect and status may be earned by performing acts of violence against other gangs, or by making other contributions to their own gang, such as selling drugs or stealing in order to bring money into the group. This respect, however, is maintained only for as long as the person remains a member and conforms to the social standards of the gang. A gang member does not have the freedom to make individual decisions or to find a place in society outside the gang.

Since gang membership meets, or at least appears to meet, basic human needs, the attraction of membership is clear. Young people coming from a disadvantaged background may not have the perspective to see the downside of gang activity: the lack of true self respect; the possibility of suffering pain, death, or grief caused by the death of a friend or relative as the result of violence; serious drug addiction; or going to prison to pay for criminal activity. Some members do "mature out" of a gang as they become older, starting a family and getting a job in order to provide for their children. But many never reach that stage, ending up in prison, getting addicted to drugs, or becoming casualties of violence.

This book explores gangs through personal experiences, from the perspectives of people who have been members of a gang or who have worked closely with gang members. The first chapter gives a variety of impressions of gang life. The second chapter discusses gang violence. In the final chapter, people who have been working to curtail gangs and gang activity describe their experiences.

SOCIAL ISSUES
FIRSTHAND

CHAPTER 1

Gang Life

Getting to Know Gangbangers

Skip Hollandsworth

In an area of Houston crowded with apartment complexes, young men can be seen standing around in groups with their hands in their pockets. The groups are dressed almost identically, but each sports a bandana of a different color, as well as other accessories.

Skip Hollandsworth, a reporter for Texas Monthly, *spent time with members of the Mara Salvatrucha gang of Salvadorans, popularly known as MS-13. In the following selection, he relates some of the highlights of their conversations. In particular, he focuses on Alex, who did his first stint at a juvenile detention center at the age of eight and was "claimed in" to the MS-13s at the age of eleven.*

On a muggy late-summer afternoon, I am sitting in my rental car in front of an apartment complex in southwest Houston. A young man named Alex, wearing a blue T-shirt and jeans, opens the passenger door and slides into the front seat. "Oh, yeah," he says, studying the windows. "This will do for a drive-by."

For a second, I'm not sure what to say. "A drive-by?" I ask. Alex throws back his head and laughs. "Señor El Bolillo, I'm just messing with you."

Señor El Bolillo: Mr. White Bread. Alex's nickname for me. He laughs again. "Do you really think I'm that *loco* to do a drive-by with an amateur?"

We are in a neighborhood that is just a ten-minute drive south of the Galleria shopping mall, one of Houston's most famous landmarks. In the seventies the area was known as Swinglesville. Dozens of sprawling apartment complexes, some of them a block long, had been built here, one right beside the other, to accommodate the horde of young, single white adults who were then coming to the city to begin their careers. The complexes were given such sophisticated names as Chateaux Carmel, Napoleon Square, Villa Royal, Sterling Point, and the Turf Club. The owners had planted crape myrtles by the front gates and offered free VCRs to renters who signed year-long leases. At one complex, a two-story disco was built next to a swimming pool.

Today the crape myrtles continue to bloom, but there are no more free VCRs—and no disco. On the walls of almost all the complexes are large banners, many written in Spanish, offering $99 move-in specials, with no credit check required. In the courtyards, where the young singles once played sand volleyball in skimpy bathing suits, young mothers in faded dresses hold babies against their hips, watching their other children kick soccer balls. Old men sit in plastic chairs on tiny balconies, drinking beer. *Paleteros* [peddlers] pedal their bicycles through the parking lots, past rusting cars, selling such treats as popsicles and spicy cucumbers out of the metal boxes tied to their handlebars.

Gangbangers on the Sidewalks

And late in the afternoons, on the sidewalks in front of many of the apartment complexes, small clusters of young males, most of them teenagers, can be seen standing around, seemingly doing nothing, their hands in their pockets. Almost all of them are wearing similar clothes: T-shirts, tennis shoes, and either neatly creased blue jeans or Dickies khaki pants that they have spray-starched themselves. Sticking out of their back pockets are patterned bandannas. Around their waists are cloth belts, the ends so long they reach down to their knees, and hanging around their necks are crosses or rosaries.

There is only one real difference in the outfits among the groups. The bandannas, belts, crosses, and rosaries on the young men in front of some of the apartment complexes are black. In front of other complexes, the color is white. In front of others, the color is blue or red. Sometimes the T-shirts and pants match the colors of their accessories. Sometimes the color of the tennis shoes is the same. The young males are gangbangers, members of such neighborhood street gangs as the Southwest Cholos, La Primera, La Tercera Crips, Somos Pocos Pero Locos, and Mara Salvatrucha, or, as it's more popularly known, MS-13. According to Houston police, they are vicious, tattooed career criminals, their lives devoted to razors, knives, and guns. They regularly rob innocent people who live in the apartment complexes. They steal cars and break into businesses. They deal drugs on street corners. And they constantly wage war with one another—fighting, maiming, killing, and dying over their turfs, their colors, and their hand signs, which have special meanings only to them.

Picking Up Alex

"Come on, let's cruise," says Alex. "Let's see the sights." He gives me a look, his eyebrows rising, and he starts laughing again. "Maybe, El Bolillo, we'll get lucky and see some bullets."

Alex, who is twenty years old, is one of the neighborhood's *veteranos*, a veteran gangbanger. Although he is just five feet three inches tall and 138 pounds, with thick, curly black hair, a little goatee covering his chin, and soft eyes the color of chocolate, people keep their distance from him. Since the age of eleven, he has been a member of the neighborhood chapter—or "clique"—of Mara Salvatrucha, which is made up of young males whose families immigrated to Houston from El Salvador and other Central American countries. By his account, he has been involved in at least a hundred—"maybe two hundred," he estimates—fistfights, knife fights, gun battles, and yes, drive-bys. Tattooed on his stomach is part of the flag of El Salvador, and on his back is a three-inch-high "MS-13": the M just below his left shoulder, the S just below his right shoulder, and the "13" in the middle. Among the tattoos on his arms is one that reads "Smile Now, Cry Later," which he says he received to commemorate the gunning down of a rival gangbanger.

And on his left wrist is a small tattoo consisting only of three dots in a triangular formation: the symbol of la vida loca. The crazy life. "The gangbanger's life," says Alex.

He points to one of the dots. "We have a saying down here that if you live la vida loca, you'll end up in the hospital." He points to the second dot. "Or you'll end up in prison." He then points to the third dot. "Or you'll end up dead."

The Enemy

I put the car into gear, and Alex tells me to turn one way, then another, until we end up on a street called Dashwood. "You see them? The *chavala?*" Alex asks, pointing to three young Hispanic males standing in front of one of the apartment complexes.

The *chavala:* slang for "the enemy." The three males are members of the Southwest Cholos, a Hispanic neighborhood gang made up mostly of young men whose parents are native-born Mexican Americans or immigrants from Mexico. With black bandannas in their back pockets, they are, to borrow a gangbanger's phrase, "showing the black rag."

"All I have to do is show them some blue, and it all starts going down," says Alex, who has a blue bandanna sticking out of his back pocket and who is also wearing a long blue belt and a blue rosary.

We pass the three Cholos—they are on the right side of the car, not far from Alex's window—and he stares at them with a surly, challenging expression: "Mad dogging," or "murder mugging," is the term that the gangbangers use to describe such a look. The Cholos, in turn, "mad dog" him.

"They know you?" I ask.

"F--- yeah, they know me, fool. Everybody knows everybody in the hood."

Suddenly nervous, I press down on the accelerator. The rental car lurches forward, and Alex bursts into laughter again.

"El Bolillo," he says, "I mean no disrespect, but you'll never get to do any drive-bys if you keep driving like that." . . .

Alex's Background

In many ways, Alex is the classic gangbanger case study. He was born in 1985, shortly after his parents moved to Houston from El Salvador and ended up in one of the southwest apartment complexes. According to Alex, his parents' marriage was stormy, and he often found himself alone, a barrio latchkey kid. "I was the smallest little f---er for my age in the hood," he says. "So I knew I had to learn to box or I wasn't going to make it."

He apparently became an outstanding boxer ("boxer" is slang for "street fighter"), so much so, he says, that he was sent off to a juvenile detention facility at the age of eight because some boy from another apartment complex had shouted, "F--- you, you El Salvadoran chicken," and Alex had gone after him with a metal rod.

He said he learned one very important lesson at the detention center: "Don't back away from anyone. If you want to talk shit to me, I'm going to talk shit back. And if you want to hit me, you better think twice, because I'm going to fight dirty. There were a bunch of *vatos* [gang members] at juvenile detention who would come up to me and say I would be a perfect boxer for their gang."

He says he was sent to juvenile detention a second time for attacking a man who had hit his mother, and when he got out, he began hanging out on the southwest Houston streets with older members of Mara Salvatrucha. "I did everything I could to impress them," he says. "I heard stories about their OGs ["Original Gangsters," a term for leaders of the gang] and the crimes they did. I heard about the drive-bys against the gangs that hated us. The OGs were my heroes."

Alex Joins the Gang

Just after his eleventh birthday, a group of OGs led him behind a dumpster at one of the apartment complexes. They took off their shirts and proceeded to beat him for a minute or two. It was Alex's initiation into Mara Salvatrucha—a process that the gangbangers call "clicking in." Alex was not allowed to fight back or make any kind of sound. At the end of the beating, the OGs pulled him to his feet and hugged him.

"You're one of us now," they said. "You're a *homito*." A homeboy.

"And how did that make you feel?" I ask.

"Man, I was part of a family. I had someone always watching my back. That meant a lot to me. I'd never known what that felt like. For me, MS was the most important thing in my life. I lived for the gang, and I was going to die for the gang."

Alex turned his room into a shrine to Mara Salvatrucha. He put the flag of El Salvador on one wall. On another wall, he put up a poster showing an angry young man, his body covered in tattoos, throwing down one of the MS-13 gang signs: His fingers twisted so that his right hand was in the shape of an M and his left hand in the shape of an S. Alex went through the neighborhood spray-painting "MS-13" on walls, and when he got a little money together, he bought his gang clothes.

Gang Clothing

For years, southwest Houston gangbangers, regardless of what gang they belong to, have been buying their clothes at the very same stores. They buy their Dickies pants either at a particular neighborhood grocery store or a nearby uniform shop. They buy their bandannas at a dollar store in the neighborhood, and they buy their cloth belts from a flea market at the intersection of Highway 59 and Westpark. At the Sharpstown Center, a nearby mall that has a notice on the front door that reads "Weapons Not Permitted on Premises," they buy what they call Gangster Nikes: black or colored Nikes with white stripes. And while they are at the mall, they head down to the jewelry stores, usually Jewelry Dog USA or TV Jewelry, to check out the crosses and rosaries.

"I love being down with the blue," he says of the clothes he wears. "All I do is talk blue. If I see a homeboy, he says, 'Wassup, niggah?' And I say, 'Just blue rag hangin', or 'It's going blue,' or 'Just throwing down the MS.'"

(For reasons I could never quite understand, all the Hispanic gangbangers greet a fellow homeboy by calling him "niggah.")

"And if you see someone wearing another rag?" I ask.

"It's an insult, a slap across my face. And when they drive past our apartment complex, where we do our chillin', that's f---ed, trying to make mess with us in our hood."

At that very moment, I'm sitting with Alex in one of those apartments he shares with two other homeboys. There is no furniture in the living room and dining room except for a couple of mattresses. In the bedroom, there is a bed and a cheap radio, which is playing MEGA 101 FM, "Latino and Proud." The apartment doesn't look as if it's been renovated since the eighties. The carpets are tattered, the walls need paint, and the kitchen refrigerator doesn't get cold. For this, the rent is $650 a month.

"This place—this apartment complex—is that important to you?" I ask, unable to keep the surprise out of my voice.

"El Bolillo," Alex says, "this is my life. This is the only life I have. I'm not going let someone f--- with my life." . . .

MS-13 Gangs

Many large cities have an MS-13 gang. Each one operates independently, and just like the Southwest Cholos, there are various cliques within each city's gang. It is true that in recent years MS-13 gang members from Central America have illegally crossed the border and gotten involved with one of the gangs already here. Many of them are more violent than the homegrown Mara Salvatruchans. Still, they haven't significantly changed the balance of gang warfare. One day, Alex took me to lunch with a young MS-13 member named Fernando who had just arrived from Guatemala. He had tattoos on his body but not on his face (when newspapers run stories about MS-13, they tend to run photos of the Central American members who are in prison and have facial tattoos), he dressed nicely, and though he couldn't speak any English, he said, as best as he could when lunch was over, "Thank you, sir," and he shook my hand.

"Is Fernando some sort of trained killer?" I later ask Alex, thinking about some of the alarmist articles I had read about MS-13.

"El Bolillo, you are such a f---ing goofy-ass *gabacho* [a pejorative term for a white person]," Alex says. "Fernando's working at a shirt embroidery shop in the neighborhood, making $6.50 an hour."

After dropping out of high school, Alex had also worked at that shop, and he's also worked for his uncle's roofing company, making $10 an hour. As far as I can tell, that's his main source of income, which allows him to pay for his rent, cell phone, and food. Alex is obviously not in the gang for the money. He has no car, he doesn't have the money for his own apartment, and he doesn't buy many clothes. When I ask him what he does for money when he's in a tight spot, he gives me one of his smiles and says, "Oh, don't worry. I know what to do."

Alex's adult criminal record is relatively skimpy: just three convictions for drug possession and one conviction for assault. A law enforcement official told me that Alex's juvenile record, which by law he could not reveal, is "far more impressive," involving a variety of thefts.

Alex Tells Stories of His Crimes

Alex regaled me with numerous stories of crimes he has committed for which he was not arrested. At the age of thirteen, he says, he stole several cars from the parking lot of the Bellaire Square apartments (a Cholos hangout) and sold them. He and other gang members, he says, broke into a Wal-Mart in a failed attempt to get into the cash registers to get money to pay for a fellow homeboy's bail.

Most of his stories, however, are about battles with rival Cholos who, in some way, have shown "disrespect" (one of Alex's favorite words). He says he started a fight with a Cholo at one of the neighborhood nightclubs by "stacking" him: using both of his hands to flash gang signs, one right after the other—similar to what a third-base coach does in baseball. (Among the signs he displays is one that shows the Cholos being shot down and rubbed out, which is almost guaranteed to provoke a brawl.) He says he was part of a team of MS-13 members who shot at a Cholo coming out of a party. (He refuses to tell me whether the Cholo was wounded or killed.) He also says he is sometimes used as the driver in the gang's drive-bys "because I know all the shortcuts and how to disappear down the back alleys."

In fact, directly below the MS-13 tattoo on his back is another tattoo that reads "El Rata"—the Rat. It's his gang nickname, which he says has little to do with his slight stature. "Once I do my business, I get away," he says. "I scurry away just like a rat from the cops, from other gangs, from anyone else who's after me. If I didn't get away, you wouldn't be talking to me. I'd have been dead a long time ago. Think about it, El Bolillo. I'm about to turn twenty-one, and I'm still on the streets. Not too many other f---ing gang bangers in the barrio can say they've been doing it as long as I have."

But the question is, How long can Alex keep doing it? During one of my trips in September to the neighborhood, I began hearing rumors that some of the Cholos had put out a hit on Alex. "There's a tag on my head, yeah, but there's always been a tag on my head," he says when I see him.

I'm not sure whether to believe the last half of his sentence. I ask him if it's true that someone shot at him the previous week. "Yeah, coming out of a convenience store off of Rampart. Someone drove by in a black car and a bullet came my way," he says. "F---ing Cholos." He then tells me he's moving from one apartment to another, just in case.

Youth Advocates Counsel Gang Kids

I originally heard about Alex from Charles Rotramel, of Youth Advocates. Every day, Rotramel has his twelve counselors travel to gang-ridden areas throughout the city to meet gang kids, and in 2004 one of them came across Alex. (There used to be other groups who did the same thing, but they now have trouble getting funded. Much of the government funding they once received goes, in the post-9/11 age, to homeland security. There is a Mayor's Anti-Gang Office, but it has only six counselors to cover the entire city. Because the Houston City Council will not devote any of the city budget to the Anti-Gang Office, except to fund two staff positions, it too has to look for grants to keep its doors open.)

To the surprise of everyone at Youth Advocates, Alex had shown up at the Youth Advocates building off Interstate 45, far from the southwest neighborhood. He said he wanted to check out the break-dancing program—and "check out the girls."

"We figured it was his way of saying that the gang life, for all its excitement, was starting to get to him," says Rotramel, who has recently moved the Youth Advocates office to southwest Houston. "You see it happen so often to so many gang kids as they start hitting their twenties. They know they are not happy, they can't sleep at night because of the stress, and they're worried that the cops or the other gangs are finally going to catch up to them. And here is one place where an option is presented to them of a life that's different—a life of pizza and listening to music and not having to think about drive-bys."

When I see Alex in September, I ask him if he's thinking that the time has come to leave.

"What do you mean, 'leave'?"

"Leave the gang," I say.

As we're having this conversation, we're walking into a neighborhood *pupuseria*, a restaurant that specializes in El Salvadoran food. Immediately the customers stop talking. I assume that they have turned silent because they realize that a member of the feared Mara Salvatrucha, showing his blue, has arrived.

"No, El Bolillo," says Alex. "They're used to gangsters. *Gabachos* never come in here."

Alex's Relationship with a Girl from a Rival Gang

He orders two beers, both at the same time. I ask him again if he thinks about leaving. But instead of answering, he tells me a story about a girl he had met a year ago. She was fourteen, known as a "Cholita"—which meant she got passed around sexually among the Cholos. "I didn't care," says Alex. "When I met her, it was a whole different story for me. My insides felt different. She knew I was carrying out assignments to get rid of Cholos, but she still cared about me. I never had anyone care about me as much as she did, and I had never cared for any girl like I did for her. I'm not lying to you. My insides felt different."

They maintained a secret relationship for several months. He borrowed, or perhaps stole (I was never able to get the truth out of him), a car and took her to an Olive Garden south of Houston near the Johnson Space Center—"the one place where I knew I wouldn't find any gangsters." He went to Jewelry Dog USA at the Sharpstown Center and bought her a fourteen-karat gold necklace with a medallion that read "LOVE." She, in turn, went to Jewelry Dog USA and bought him a grill—a metallic mouthpiece, popular among rappers, that had MS-13 written across the front plate.

When a friend heard about the relationship, she told him it was just like Romeo and Juliet. Alex, who knew nothing about the ill-fated love affair [in the play by William Shakespeare], says he went to a video store and rented three different versions of the movie. "And we watched them all. All of them. One with Leonardo DiCaprio, another with somebody else, and a real old one. That one was my favorite."

"A *veterano* with MS-13 has watched *Romeo and Juliet*," I say quietly.

"Oh yeah, El Bolillo, and I also got that damn *West Side Story*. Too much f---ing music."

There's a silence, and Alex finishes one of the beers. He then returns to the story and tells me that the girl's mother learned about him. She realized that if the Cholos got wind of the relationship, which they inevitably would, her daughter would be killed. One day, the mother and daughter disappeared. "They went to Central America somewhere" he says. "I could never find out. Right before they left, I told my girl that we were going to get married and leave Houston and start a new life with a baby. I told her we could go to North Carolina."

"Why North Carolina?" I ask.

"I've never been there, but I know it's far away. I told her I'd always wear a shirt so no one would see the tattoos—so no one would find me. I cried like a baby when she was taken away from me."

After a Fight

A couple of weeks later I return to southwest Houston and head to the apartment where Alex is staying. When I walk in, he is hanging with three of his homeboys. Blaring out of a boom box is a rap song that sounds like gunfire. "We're survivors, still standing," the rapper shouts in Spanish.

Alex isn't looking good. His face and body are bruised. One of his lips is puffy. There's a fresh scar across one of the tattoos on his left arm.

"F---ing Cholos," he says.

He tells the other homeboys and me that he had been walking alone the previous afternoon down Rampart Street toward the Bellaire Square apartments. A group of Cholos had driven by in an old Lincoln, the front seat pushed all the way back. One Cholo had leaned his head out the window and shouted, "*Cholos controla!*"

"F--- you, you punk!" another Cholo had shouted.

"Then what, Alex?" asks Julian, one of the homeboys. Julian is only thirteen years old. He was "clicked in" to the gang a couple of months earlier, and he worships Alex. At his middle school, he proudly tells other students that he is part of Alex's "crew" and that he is doing "missions" with him. (When I had first met Julian, I had asked him what those missions were. He had grinned confidently and said in as forceful a voice as he could muster for someone who had barely reached puberty, "Mr. Reporter, you don't want to know what we do after dark. You really don't want to know.")

"What did you do, Alex?" Julian asks again. I realize I'm holding my breath. I want Alex to tell us he kept his head down, refusing to take the bait. I want to believe that Alex has not traveled too far down a certain road to be able to retrace his steps.

But Alex says, "I did what I had to do for the gang, my *homito*. I threw down. Chunked them our sign."

According to Alex, the driver of the Cholos' car hit the brakes and everybody came after him. Alex started running, but one of the Cholos was far faster than Alex expected. He pushed Alex to the ground. Another Cholo raced up and began kicking him in the ribs.

"But the f---ing *putos* didn't see my knife," says Alex, El Rata. "I got the leg of one of them, then I slashed some motherf---er's arm. That got them the f--- outta my face. And then I was gone. Ran down an alley and was gone."

"Now what?" asks Julian, his eyes gleaming.

Alex shrugs and stares at Julian. "What do you mean, 'Now what?' They come back at us. And we come back at them."

Alex shrugs again, and just like that, he seems ready to talk about something else. He looks over at me leaning against a bare wall, taking notes. He gives me a smile. "Hey, El Bolillo, take us out to eat on your credit card," he says. "Come on, you know we need our fruits and vegetables."

We head out the door of the apartment and walk down the stairs and into the parking lot to my car. Instinctively, he pauses to see who else might be in the parking lot. He looks to the left, then to the right. He looks toward the street to see what cars are coming his way.

"Come on, El Bolillo. Let's cruise."

The Ups and Downs
of Gang Life

Jorge Fuentes, as told to Celeste Fremon

Jorge Fuentes describes himself as a member of the Clarence Street Locos (CLS), a Mexican American gang in East Los Angeles. His gang name is Wizard. In this selection, recorded by Celeste Fremon, Wizard talks about some of his family history, his rationale for joining a gang, and the reasons he wants to leave gang life. He also talks about "G," which is the gang members' nickname for Father Greg Boyle, a Catholic priest who works among Los Angeles gang members and encourages them to make the best of themselves. After this selection was written, Father Greg helped Wizard to get a job interview, and Wizard began a career in television production.

My name's Jorge Fuentes, but they call me Wizard. I have one brother and three sisters. I'm the youngest one in the family. My dad's my real dad. He's an alcoholic. The doctors say he's going to die from the drinking, but he won't stop.

When I was growing up, I was in my own little world. I was a wild kid. I was always talking back to teachers.

An Abusive Father

When I got older, they kept on putting me in the gifted classes. I liked that. But when they have you in those classes they expect you to do a lot of homework. There was no place to do it at my house. I used to always blame it on my dad. He's kind of violent. He used to beat up my mom. He'd say things to me—things like I wasn't his son and stuff. And call me all kinds of names. I used to leave and just kick it outside; take a deep breath before I got mad and try to hit him.

When I grew up, I'd leave when he started drinking. But then I'd come home and find out what he'd done, and I'd get mad. I always wanted to fight him. I wanted to take out my anger, once and for all. I never did. Some nights I used to break out in tears because I wanted to hit him so badly and I couldn't, because my mom would come out and say not to step onto his level because he was an alcoholic; that I should understand, and this and that. He'd find any little excuse to go drink. Then he used to blame it on me. Say it was my fault. It was not my fault. He was an alcoholic.

Then I started drinking too.

My mom stayed with him because she's from Mexico, and in Mexico they're not as into women's rights. In Mexico you stick by the man and that's how it has to be. No matter what the man says or does. She's a good mother. Very understanding. No matter what I've said or done, she's always stood by me.

Friend in the Gang

Ghost's my best friend. We understand each other. When something happens, I try to tell him not to think about it the hard way, but to think about it in a way that's good for him. And when I get upset or all flared up, he tells me not to think about it.

I got courted into the neighborhood [initiated into a gang] five years ago, at fourteen. I was going to get into another gang—Cuatro Flats. They used to be called Pico Stoners. They said to me, "We're going to court you in." I said, "If you jump me in, you're going to be mugging me. You're not going to be courting me in." But then CSL [Clarence Street Locos] said they'd have somebody fight me, one on one. So I said, "Okay. Bring 'em on."

Sometimes at night I think, "Why did I get in?" I got in because I thought it was fun. But it was very disappointing. I wish I could go back to school and not be in a gang. There ain't nothing good in it. I wish I had an education. But if I wasn't in a gang, I'm pretty sure I would have been getting jumped all the time. So things would have gone wrong either way—in a gang or not in a gang, I would've gotten into trouble either way.

A lot of guys don't have the guts to say, "I'm going to stop banging." They got no will power. They're like little toys being controlled. I try to make some of the younger guys, on both sides, understand. But they don't listen. They think they're just having fun. They're just going through what I was going through. I thought I was having fun too.

The Gang Begins Using Guns

I'd like to give all these gang members one more last chance. The chance would be to take away all the things you regret that you did—whatever that is—and see what happens. I'd do it for everybody in all the neighborhoods. See what they do with the chance. Also, if I had a fairy godmother I'd want her to take away the guns. You know when the guns got introduced to us? It was when that movie, *Colors*, came out. The movie didn't make it happen. But the movie introduced a whole new concept. When the Mexican gangs saw all the fighting happening between the Crips and the Bloods, we said, "Damn! We ain't going to stay without a gun 'cause we could die!" In about a week, everybody had guns and deaths were happening.

I've blasted. I don't hide it. And I've hit somebody more than once. They all lived. I don't know if any one of 'em knew it was me. The thing that leads up to it is anger. Your friends dying. Your friends getting shot or stabbed. Then—damn!—you're so mad you want to get revenge. The first one to die from our neighborhood was Toker's twin brother, Armando.

We were so young. We were in the park kicking it when some guys popped out with guns. We all ran, but he slipped. And when he got up again, they shot 'im. BAM. Everybody was crying.

The second one was Shotgun. He was cool, always joking around to make you laugh. That's why it really hurt. He used to shoot a lot. That was during the time when I used to hold the guns. You can't be unpredictable and take care of the guns. I guess they wanted me to do it because I was very trustable.

I'll tell you how you hide a gun. You should hide it in the most obvious place because people are too dumb to look there. Like in the dashboard of a car. Or inside the speaker box. There's a really powerful magnet inside a car stereo speaker box. You can just put the gun in and it'll stick easily because of the magnet. It won't rattle or nothing. Or you can put it in the front of the car right near the radiator—there's a little space. Make sure the wires are on top, so the gun won't jump out. It's really easy. Even now, if I want a gun, I just dial seven numbers and it'll come.

Stopping Banging Because of His Kids

I knew I needed to stop banging for a long time. I knew it in my heart, but I still needed to let the doors open, and let it come into my head. I stopped banging for my two kids. I adore kids. The homies got mad at me one time, because they said I wasn't going to the 'hood often enough. I said, "You gonna take care of my kid at night or what?" Pretty soon we had fists flying all over the place.

You could say that technically I *haven't* stopped banging. I don't blast, but I still go to see what the homies are doing— just to kick it with 'em. At one time, when I was a lot younger, right when I very first got in, we were so violent, we were so *low*, we were so desperate for fights, that we used to go around jumping people. I feel embarrassed even to say this. I mean we'd jump *men*. And sometimes we'd steal their money. I look back on that now and I feel really bad. I mean, they'd worked hard for their money. And for some hoodlum just to come, and jump 'em, and take their money away, when they were just going to the market to buy stuff for their wife and family and kids—that's low. That's terrible. When I think about that, I get mad at myself. But what am I going to do? Sock myself? I wish I could go back and make up for that. But I can't.

There was a time when I had a gun. G [Father Greg Boyle] heard about it and he got mad. He tried to get me to give it to him. He kept saying that a real man would give it up. When I wouldn't give it up, he was very disappointed. I said, "I'll become a man, G. It'll just take a little while."

One thing about me, I may have an attitude, but I'm not a hypocrite. I don't lie. Lying just makes you look dumb. I told G what I'd done, one time. I said, "I shot this many people," and I told him a number. He just looked at me and smiled. He didn't believe me. And I thought, "Oh well, at least I got it off my chest."

Calmed by a Priest

G calms everybody. He always tells me what it takes to be a man. He tells you the same thing so many times, it starts going in, little by little. We don't mind him cussing at us. We understand. He's like a father—to me—to a lot of people. He does everything a parent is supposed to do. He lectures you. He loves you. He tries to help you.

G was the person who told me that I was an alcoholic. "You drink to get drunk," he said. "I bet you pass out." My eyes started getting all watery. I was realizing when he was saying it, that there was no way I could say it wasn't true.

The saddest thing in my life is when I'm drunk. Drinking calms me down. But when I look at myself, I'm scared to become like my dad.

In ten years I want to be living somewhere far from where I live now. I want to have a nice job and live with my kids and stuff. And then I want to come back to the projects for a visit and see what everyone is doing. I want to talk to the people who hated me once, who wanted to kill me once. I want to see my friends. I'd love to talk to everybody and say, "Hey! What's up?" To see who's still playing that stupid game. And who understood, and stopped.

I'm planning to move to El Paso soon with my lady and kids because if I stay around here I'm afraid I'd get into blasting again, like I did when I was young. I don't want to do that again. But I don't trust myself.

In terms of a job, I could do anything. You tell me how to do it one time, I can do it, no matter what it is. I'd be happy with any kind of job. I'm not really picky.

I hope I have a happy life. Whenever there's two ways to walk—if one way is the long, safe way, and the other way is pure fences—I always have to go through the fences. But I guess I'm lucky. 'Cause I'm still right here living.

Choosing Not to Join a Gang

Anonymous

A high school boy, who chooses to remain anonymous and does not use his friends' real names, has managed to walk a fine line, being friends with gang members but not actually joining a gang. In this article, he describes his view of the gang life, noting in particular two instances of gang violence that he witnessed. On one occasion, a new boy in school claimed to be a member of the Crips but actually was associated with the rival gang, the Bloods. Both gangs were offended by his deception and proceeded to beat him up. In another instance, the author witnessed a boy, Ramon, being "squared in," or initiated, to the Crips. In order to prove his strength and loyalty, Ramon was beaten for twenty seconds by one gang member. Then a second member joined in the beating for twenty seconds, then a third. The boys continued to beat him even after Ramon collapsed to the ground, bruised and bloody. When the beating was over, they welcomed Ramon into the gang. He became a proud gang member. The author objects to the violence, but he still manages to maintain friendships with members of the Crips.

When I was in 8th grade, all my friends started joining the Crips gang. They bragged about how cool they were, and they made gang life look so easy and fun. I hung out with them to learn more and just to be able to say I hung out with gang members. I liked being friends with them—for protection and to be cool. But I also made sure I didn't join the gang.

I realized what my friends were and what I was not. They'd been brought up in environments where they had to be in a gang to survive. I grew up in a good home with my mom and brother, and I'd encountered fewer obstacles than they had. Though I wondered what it would be like to be in a gang, I knew I couldn't handle gang life. Some of the things gangs do, like robbery, murders and hustling, just weren't for me.

None of my friends ever directly approached me about joining because I always told them that hanging out with them was as far as I would go. My friends respected my refusal to join because, except for actually being in the gang, I fit right in with them. I even fought with them whenever they got into a beef, so they knew I was a real friend and not just a tag-along. For a little while I worried I was in too deep, fighting with the Crips against rival gangs, but I was careful not to go any further than that.

Security Guards in Gangs

Now I'm a junior in high school and I'm still friends with gang members. I'm comfortable with my role and my friends are too, so I don't face much pressure to join. But I see a lot of my classmates being pressured in my high school. I see blue bandannas, the color of the Crips, all the time in my school. I see blue beads around people's wrists and necks and the letter C (for Crips) thrown up in every direction in the hallways.

Almost everybody in my school has some kind of gang affiliation, even the security guards. Many of the guards are Crips and they greet students who are gang members by "piecing" them (doing the gang handshake). They even yell out the Crips calls, like "Co-rip" and "Blat killa" (a dis to the Bloods, a rival gang).

Usually the Crips and the Bloods hang out together at my school, and they don't have problems with each other. This is common in a lot of high schools, according to my friends who are gang members. Even though the gangs are sworn enemies, they're usually about peace in the school building. They have the occasional rumble in the hallway, but for the most part they get along.

But that doesn't mean there isn't violence. One day during my sophomore year, a freshman named Kellz transferred in from another school. When Kellz noticed that our school was mainly Crips territory, he foolishly pretended to be a Crip.

Beat-Down at School

A week after Kellz came, a Crip named Speed asked him what set he was with. A set is a division of a gang based on neighborhood or street, sort of like precincts to the police. They were in the lunchroom, and I joined the crowd of students that had started to build around them.

Kellz answered, "Original Gangsta Crip" and it just so happened that was Speed's set. Speed immediately knew he was lying. Kellz tried to apologize, but to no avail. He was so scared I could see it in his face.

Then it got even crazier. The whole time he'd been claiming to be a Crip, he was actually a Blood. We found out when somebody from his neighborhood said they'd seen him around with the Bloods. The Bloods didn't take too kindly to the news either. Eventually almost every gang member in the school pummeled him. The Crips beat him up for being a Blood pretending to be a Crip, and the Bloods beat him up because he'd been afraid to admit he was a Blood.

The Squaring In

That reassured me that I'd made the right decision not to join a gang. But what made me even more sure that gang life wasn't for me was when I witnessed my first and last initiation for a new Crips member.

One day last year, I was walking with some Crip friends and they told me they were about to square somebody in. I didn't know what that meant. My friend explained that it's when the gang recruits a new member by beating him down to make him prove he's strong enough to be in the gang.

There was a dead end behind the park where the new recruit, Ramon, met up with the Crips to be squared in. I was cool with Ramon, and I decided to watch to see how it worked.

A Painful Initiation

First Ramon fought one of my homeboys for 20 seconds. Twenty seconds later, another gang member joined, and then another every 20 seconds after that. The rule was that if Ramon fell to his knees at any point, he'd have to start all over with the first guy.

Soon there were three guys fighting Ramon at once. I could hear each blow connecting to various parts of his body, the worst of them on his head. Eventually he fell to the ground in the fetal position, blood all over his face and bruises everywhere on his arms and legs. He hadn't even made it to the fourth gang member, so they didn't bother to pick him up and start over. They just began stomping on his head and all over his body.

Ramon's face was a mixture of regret, fear and pain. Even more terrifying were the looks on the faces of the Crips as they beat him senseless. They were smiling and laughing like it was funny. They seemed to be enjoying it. "Get the f--- up!" they yelled at him as he fell. One of the boys beating him senseless was his brother.

When it was all said and done, Ramon looked dazed. The gang members tried to help him up, but he kept falling. While they waited for him to get himself together, they congratulated each other and talked about who'd beat him the worst.

Ramon finally got up and they all congratulated him for fighting his best and told him that he was down with them. He couldn't even talk. I left after that and all I could do was think about it for the rest of the night. Any thoughts I'd had of joining a gang died then and there. I was so glad that I'd had the presence of mind to not join.

A Fine Line

The next week, Ramon came to school showing off his new lifestyle. He wouldn't stop talking about it, and he was walking around like nobody could touch him. It was as if he didn't even remember what had happened to him the week before. After that, he started hanging out with the cool kids and getting into fights, and people respected him.

From what I see from my friends, the main reason they turn to gang life is peer pressure. I think Ramon joined because he didn't want to disappoint his friends. It can be hard to say no to people you've known your whole life. My friend Jay told me he became a Crip because he was pressured by his whole block and his neighborhood. He also told me he felt uncomfortable by himself and wanted protection.

I understand wanting people to protect you just in case you need some help, but I don't know if joining a gang makes anything better. Once you're in one, you probably need even more protection than you did before.

I still spend most of my time with friends who are in gangs. I know there's a pretty fine line between hanging out with a gang and joining one. But it's a line I've made clear to myself and my friends, and I'm not going to cross it.

Life Turned Around by Reading the Bible

Jeremiah Utley

When Jeremiah Utley was twelve years old, a gang member ran by his house, with a police officer running behind in pursuit. The gang member dropped his gun behind a bush and Utley retrieved it and hid it in an alley. When the man came back looking for his gun, Utley gave it to him. The man was a member of a gang called the Unknown Vice Lords. He took Utley under his wing and Utley began selling drugs and later became a gang member. Utley enjoyed the money he was making selling drugs, but it wasn't long until he was arrested for stealing a car.

While he was in jail, Utley picked up a Bible and began reading it. He came to the story about Saul, a man who had been killing Christians until his life was turned around by an encounter with Jesus. Utley identified with Saul and prayed that his life could change, too. He left the gang and was helped through his experience in Boot Camp (a prison rehabilitation program) by members of a group called Youth for Christ. The following selection is Utley's story of his mistakes and the conversion that started him on a different life path.

With my legs slightly spread and feet planted in the middle of the street, I aimed my revolver at the gray car speeding toward me. The seconds ticked by slowly as I waited for the right moment, confident I'd shoot the driver between the eyes and dive out of the way before he ran me down.

That moment never came. Before I pulled the trigger, I glanced over my shoulder and saw a police car coming at me from behind. Getting revenge on a rival gang member suddenly didn't matter. I couldn't risk getting arrested again. I darted off of the street, looking for someplace to hide.

I was only 19 and had already been in jail. If the police caught me, I was bound to end up behind bars again—but for a much longer time. My whole life was headed nowhere but down.

A Big Mistake at Age 12

It wasn't like I woke up one morning and said, "This is the day I'll destroy my life." I'd been raised by good, churchgoing parents. I was always a pretty decent kid. But one day I made a very bad decision. I was 12 at the time.

It was a pretty ordinary summer afternoon. Engines rumbled as cars slowly passed my house. Rap beats blared from boom boxes. The shouts and giggles of children at play could be heard up and down the street.

My friend and I sat in the front yard playing a game of marbles. As I knelt on the lawn, poised to flip a large marble with my thumb, I glanced toward the street and saw a guy sprinting hard. He was being chased by a police officer. The guy darted across a neighbor's yard, dropping something that looked like a gun. He then disappeared from sight, with the officer still running after him.

Always full of curiosity, I crossed the street so I could get a good look at what the guy had dropped. There it was, steel-gray body and black handgrip. I looked at it for a few seconds, then picked it up. I'd never held a gun before. It was kind of heavy, big and powerful-feeling. I carried it back across the street to show to my friend. "What will we do with it?" he asked.

I shrugged my shoulders and told him I was going to hide it in a trashcan in the alley. After I dropped it in the trash, we went back to the front yard as if nothing had happened.

Meeting a Gang Member

Later that afternoon, my friend went home and I continued to play outside. Around suppertime, a man came walking up my street. It was the guy who'd dropped the gun! He stopped in front of my house and looked at me. I avoided his eyes.

He stood there a moment, then asked, "Did you see what happened?"

I took a deep breath.

He knows I saw him, I thought. What would he do if I lied to him? I wondered. Then I had another thought. What will he do if I tell him the truth?

I swallowed hard, mumbled something about what I'd seen and then led him to the back alley. I showed where I'd put the gun.

"I wasn't going to keep it," I said nervously.

"You didn't do nothing wrong," he said without any anger in his voice. In fact, he sounded like he admired me for thinking so quickly—and, I realized later, for keeping him out of trouble. "It's OK. You're smart. I need smart kids. Let's take a walk." Without my parents or any of my siblings around, I didn't think twice about walking down the street with this stranger. He seemed kind of cool and scary, all at the same time.

He explained that he was a member of the Unknown Vice Lords. He said his gang needed smart kids like me for lookouts. He told me I could make good money working for him.

As we walked back to my house, he said, "Don't give me an answer now. Just think about it. I'll come back."

A few days later, he showed up again—this time he pulled up in his big fancy Buick Regal. We talked a little. As I stood there leaning on his shiny car, I thought, I want a cool car like this someday. After he talked to me for a while, he invited me to take a ride with him. Again, my family wasn't around, so I decided a little ride wouldn't do any harm.

Selling Drugs

He drove me to Sportmart and bought me a chrome bike with black mag wheels! He explained that I could use the bike to help his gang watch for cops during drug sales. I couldn't believe my luck. I was the youngest of 11 children and my parents couldn't afford a bike like this. Being a lookout suddenly seemed real cool. I had no problem saying yes.

Knowing I couldn't take the bike home, I hid it at a friend's house. Before long, I was making about $150 a day as a lookout. I bought brand-name clothes, shoes and other stuff I'd always wanted. For me, buying things was like an addiction. The more stuff I got, the more I wanted. I hid everything from my parents—especially my new life of selling drugs, buying high-end stuff and owning two tricked-out cars. By the time I reached sophomore year of high school, I had a lot to hide. I was no longer just a lookout. I'd decided to sell drugs so that I could make more money.

I was making close to $2,000 a week selling weed when I decided to join the Unknown Vice Lords. Doing so allowed me to expand my drug-selling territory. Life seemed great.

Getting Arrested

One afternoon I forced a guy out of his car and was planning to use it to track down a guy from a rival gang. Things went bad—really fast. I got in a high-speed car chase with the police and ended up arrested and charged with robbery and assault. Although I faced the possibility of a serious sentence, I only spent about two weeks in jail and got two years probation.

Suddenly, my hidden life was out in the open. I think my parents had suspected I was doing some bad stuff, but now they knew it. Dad was angry. Mom cried a lot. They both prayed hard. So did the people in my church. During my two weeks in jail, I even asked for God's help. Desperation will do that to you. But I wasn't serious—I just wanted to get out of trouble. Soon I was back to my old ways.

Then came the day I could have murdered a man, or been killed by his speeding car.

After I darted off the street that day, I sprinted to a friend's house and found an unlocked door. No one seemed to be home, so I quickly hid my gun and shut myself in a closet. After a few minutes, I heard shouting and feet shuffling—very close by. Then the closet door swung open and I was pushed down on my face and handcuffed. I was taken to the police station and interrogated.

In County Jail

When the metal bars clanked behind me at the county jail, I stared down the dimly lit hall that led to my cell. Prisoners with hardened, angry faces stared at me. This became my "home" for the next seven months until my trial. The charges against me included one for carrying an illegal firearm.

As I sat in my jail cell, regret and guilt overwhelmed me. I didn't want to spend my life selling drugs, running from the law, in and out of jail. I wanted out—not just out of jail, but out of the gang, too. That seemed impossible. People just didn't quit gangs.

Reading the Bible

One night I couldn't sleep, so I started looking through a Bible. Although I'd been brought up in the church, I never paid much attention to this old, hard-to-follow book. But this Bible was easy to understand. It was also interesting. Before long, I came to a story about a Christian-killer named Saul. One day he met Jesus, discovered God's love, found forgiveness, and started living for God. Here was a really awful man who was able to leave his old way of life.

Maybe there is hope, I thought. Maybe I can change. I shut my eyes and prayed long and hard, asking God to help me out of the mess I'd made of my life.

Miracles Happen

As I waited for my trial, I kept reading the Bible. I even started talking to other prisoners about God. I also talked to fellow gang members who were serving time. I told them I wanted to follow God and leave the gang. Their response surprised me. They said that if I was being real, I could quit the gang. But if I was messing with them, I'd pay for it.

That was miracle number one. Then came the second miracle: sentencing. Although I'd faced a maximum 21-year sentence, it was reduced to four months in Boot Camp! Boot Camp is a tough program that seeks to rehabilitate young criminals through hard work and lots of discipline.

At Boot Camp I met two men who were with a juvenile justice ministry run by Youth for Christ—an organization that tells teenagers about a relationship with Jesus. They taught me so much about living for Christ. They stuck with me and helped me get my life together.

Since I finished Boot Camp, I've had a lot of opportunities to tell my story, I want people to know the choices they make do matter and can have serious consequences, like the choice I made at age 12. I also want everyone to know that God can change anybody.

No one is too lost for God to find. I ought to know. He found me.

Released from Prison and Adjusting to the Outside World

Reymundo Sanchez

Reymundo Sanchez grew up in Chicago and became a member of the Latin Kings gang. He got involved in gang activities, including selling drugs. When he was twenty-one years old, he was arrested for possession of cocaine and sentenced to prison. In this excerpt from his book Once a King, Always a King, *he describes his transition back into the world after serving his sentence. When he left prison, he was sent to a work release center, where he was expected to live, attend Narcotics Anonymous meetings, and get a job. He talks about how differently people reacted to him when he was wearing a suit to apply for the job, how inadequate he felt when completing the application, and his joy when he successfully passed three required tests and was given a data entry job at the University of Illinois, Chicago.*

In early fall I was taken by van to a work release center on Roosevelt and Ashland Avenues in Chicago. I wasn't handcuffed on the ride there, and I wore street clothes that [my friend] Lilly had brought me for the occasion. At the work release center, I was far enough away from the neighborhood to feel safe, but close enough to where I felt like I was back in the 'hood. That, along with the cold weather beginning to set in, made the temptations of street life easy to ignore.

At the work release center, I was to start the process of integrating myself back into society as a law-abiding citizen. I wore street clothes all the time and was known by my name instead of by a prison number. I was trusted to go out in public on my own to seek employment and to attend Narcotics Anonymous (NA) meetings, which I was mandated to attend.

Facing the Past

The NA meetings were held at St. Elizabeth Hospital, in what was once Spanish Lords' 'hood, and also where I had originally been introduced to gang involvement. The Lords and the Spanish Cobras violently shared the Tuley School area. The Spanish Lords could no longer hang out at Tuley as safely as they once had. From the work release center, I took a bus that headed north on Ashland Avenue. I got off on Chicago Avenue and took the bus there to Western Avenue. From there I would take the Western Avenue bus to Hirsch Street, where I got off and walked to the NA meeting. Although this route seemed long and complicated, it allowed for the least chance of running into any gangbangers. Once I got off the bus to walk to the hospital, I always felt nervous about the possibility of running into any members of the Cobras, or even the Lords, for that matter. Time and time again, I walked past the mouth of the alley where Afro had been gunned down when I was getting my first taste of gang life at age twelve. Afro was a sixteen-year-old member of the Spanish Lords, shot to death by the Spanish Cobras as he went to buy beer for some other kids and me. We waited for him sitting on the steps of a closed-in porch about fifty feet away from where the shooting took place. I could have avoided walking past there now, but for some reason I didn't. Each time, I looked down into the alley and saw the faded spray-painted "R.I.P. Afro" on the very spot where he had died. I saw myself staring down at Afro's bloodied body, feeling nothing. I saw myself running toward the end, trying to get home before the police showed up. I realized now that having to walk past there, where all the madness of my past had started, was by far more therapeutic than the NA meetings. I also began to realize how lucky I was to have avoided Afro's fate.

A former Latin King with indirect ties to my past conducted the NA meetings. Although he didn't remember ever meeting me, he told me he knew many Kings and Queens from the Kedzie and Armitage (KA) area, including Loco, then leader of the KA Latin Kings; Loca, the older woman who took me as a lover and whose son died in my arms; and even Morena, the murdered Latin Queen who cared enough to show me how to survive on the streets, even if that meant being a ruthless gangbanger. Having him as my counselor allowed me to go to St. Elizabeth, have him sign my participation form, and then leave to go see Lilly without actually attending the meeting.

Lilly now lived on Damen and Division with a friend and her boyfriend. She had had a falling-out with Loca while I was in jail and had stopped working for her. Because of that, Lilly lost her apartment, so she sold everything except the bed and moved in with a friend. Lilly would often be waiting for me outside St. Elizabeth's when I arrived there. Lilly's roommates were watching television and getting high on just about every visit. To avoid the temptation of joining them, I locked myself in Lilly's bedroom and had sex with her. In essence, my visits to Lilly's were like conjugal visits. I would arrive, we'd go into her room and have sex, and then I would leave. We never said very much to each other.

Applying for a Job

During my third week at the work release center, one of the counselors gave me some information regarding temporary data entry positions at the University of Illinois at Chicago [UIC]. He thought that my brief employment at the University of Chicago and the computer skills I had gained at Shawnee made me a prime candidate for the job. They would be accepting applications that upcoming Monday. The counselor had already taken the liberty of making arrangements for me to be there. "Call your people and tell them to bring you a shirt and tie and some good slacks," the counselor advised as he handed me his office phone. I called Lilly and told her what the counselor said. That weekend she showed up at the work release center with a black two-piece suit, a white shirt, and a tie with black and blue designs on it. She also brought me a pair of dress shoes and socks to go along with the clothes. The clothes and shoes fit perfectly; either it was a sign of good things to come, or Lilly knew me a lot more that I had imagined.

People React Differently if You're Wearing a Suit

Monday I left the center dressed as I had never dressed before in my life. I felt uncomfortable, yet confident and mature. What I liked most about my attire were the looks of approval and respect I got from the passengers on the bus I took. I didn't see the customary looks of fear and nervousness. People just looked my way and smiled politely, some even said, "Good morning." As I approached an empty seat next to an older woman, she moved her bag away from the seat to make room for me instead of further occupying it, as I was used to people doing. I sat next to her and said thank you. "It's quite all right. Are you having a good morning?" the lady said. "Yes, I am," I responded. I didn't know what to make of all the politeness directed my way. I'm sure the lady would have wanted to have a brief conversation based on absolutely nothing to help kill time until she reached her destination, but I sat there quietly. I began to think about how she, and the rest of the passengers on that bus, would react if they found out that I was a convicted felon. I knew that the nice clean suit made all the difference in how they reacted. "Have a nice day," the lady said as I got up and started for the exit. "You too. Thank you," I responded.

I will never forget that day. The reaction from the other passengers on that bus still makes me smile and helps me keep my priorities in order. Although I'm well aware that some of the world's biggest felons wear suits on a daily basis, I'm still satisfied with not projecting a fear of violence upon those around me.

Filling Out the Application

I arrived at the University of Illinois at Chicago's employment office about twenty minutes before the appointed time. The receptionist gave me the application so I could fill it out while I waited. This would be the first time in my life that I actually completed a job application on my own. Loca's sister had filled out most of the application for the University of Chicago job I once had. I had never realized before how tough it was to write about myself, especially when I had very little information of positive substance to provide.

I became extremely nervous as I glanced down the application. When I got to the education portion, I began to doubt myself. Had it not been for the possibility of being taken out of the work release program and sent back to prison, I probably would have walked out without completing the application. The previous employment section further increased my self-doubt. Here I was, a man in perfect physical condition, in his twenties, and all the work experience I could account for was a year at the University of Chicago. It didn't help that the reason for leaving was "I quit." Then came the most embarrassing and anxiety-building question on the application. Have you ever been convicted of a felony? If yes, explain.

That question blew my mind. I slumped in my chair and just stared at it. Never in my wildest dreams did I think that I would have to share the fact that I was a convicted felon with the rest of the world. I stared at the "If yes, explain," and saw a clear reason why they would never hire me if I checked this. But I also knew that the address I provided as my place of residence was the work release center, and I would surely be caught in a lie if I chose to answer "no." As far as I was concerned, the consequence of choosing either was that I would not be considered for a job. Answering yes meant that the person reviewing the application would look at me and see a criminal instead of an applicant. The date of the conviction would alert them that I was on work release or on parole. Either way, they would know that I was the property of the Illinois correctional system. "You can go in now," said the receptionist, waking me up from my nervous daydream. I quickly checked the "No" box of the felony question, signed the application, and handed it to her.

I felt so humiliated looking at a work application and not having anything positive to put on it. I was incredibly embarrassed to be in my twenties and have no work experience or education other than a G.E.D. In fact, had I shared the life experiences that the application sought to discover, I would have painted the picture of a good-for-nothing bum. Up until then my only major accomplishment was straightening out my thought process via incarceration.

I have never forgotten the shame I felt that day, just as I'll never forget that at twenty-something I was elated to land a six-dollar-an-hour job. (Each and every time I fill out or see a job application I feel the same way I felt that day, especially when I read that question that still sends chills up my spine: "Have you ever been convicted of a felony?" I still check "no.")

Passing the Tests

The receptionist took the application and led me to a room that held about eight computers. She instructed me to sit wherever I wanted and wait for someone to come in and see me. In the next fifteen minutes, five other individuals joined me in that room. Then a woman came in, closed the door behind her, and announced herself as the test administrator. She explained that we would be taking several tests we needed to pass in order to be considered for the data entry position. We would be taking a reading and comprehension test, an alphanumeric code memory test, and a typing speed test. We had to score ninety percent or higher on the first two tests and had to accurately type at least twenty-five words per minute. The computer we were taking the tests on would tell us that we passed or failed at the end of each test. The woman advised us that, if we failed one, to continue and take the others, and that an opportunity to retake the test we had failed would be given at another date.

I passed all three tests and was surprised that I got a perfect score on the reading and comprehension portion. I stared at the computer screen, looking at my passing scores with a wicked grin on my face and a feeling of superiority. Even if I wasn't hired, I would definitely leave UIC feeling that I had accomplished something. Only two other applicants passed all three tests. The three that didn't pass were dismissed, and the rest of us were told to report to the admissions and records office the next day at eight in the morning. We were advised to arrive at least fifteen minutes early and to bring identification with us.

Getting Ready for the New Job

I left the UIC employment office feeling happier than I had ever felt in my life. The six dollars and twenty-five cents an hour this temporary position paid represented one of my greatest accomplishments. I walked toward the bus stop in a fantasy world built on the good things to come. At the center I immediately announced, "I got the job, I got the job," when I saw the counselor who had told me about the position. He shook my hand, congratulated me, and asked when I would start. I told him that I would start work the next day. As I spoke, it dawned on me; I had no means of identification.

"Oh, shit, man," I said as I sat on a chair in the office. A sudden feeling of doom engulfed me. I began to get the feeling that I had been put on this earth to suffer failure after failure, with only teasers for happiness. "What's wrong?" the counselor asked. "They want me to show up with IDs tomorrow," I said, "and I don't have any." "Come on, let's go get you some IDs," the counselor said as he put some files away and got up from behind his desk. He pulled my file from a cabinet and off we went.

The counselor took me to get a State of Illinois picture ID and a social security card. That's all the identification I needed to present at UIC. On the ride to and from getting the IDs, the counselor explained the rules that came along with being an employed inmate at the work release center. He told me that I would have to sign over my check to the center every payday. They would provide transportation and lunch money until my first paycheck, and then I would have to pay my own way. He also told me that a small amount would be taken from my paycheck as payment for room and board. Also, an allowance would be granted to me for clothes and other personal items. The remainder of my pay would be put into a savings account that would be given to me in full upon my successful completion of the work release program. This procedure was set up to teach me the responsibility of taking care of my finances and myself. I had no problem with the rules; I was just eager to start a new life.

Starting Work

On Monday, I showed up at UIC confident that I would do a good job. I showed up at seven-thirty in the morning and waited for the woman who would be my new supervisor to arrive. While I waited, I filled out a W-4 and had copies of my IDs made. When the supervisor arrived, I was all ready to go. While the other two applicants waited for their paperwork, I had already started training for the job at hand.

My job was to key student grades into the university database. It was a simple procedure. All I had to do was call up the student record by ID number, fill in the blanks with a letter grade for the respective class, and hit the enter key to update the record. I caught on quickly and did a good, efficient job. Overtime was available, so I worked ten hours a day for the first two weeks. I loved my job at UIC and did not look forward to the end of this temporary assignment.

CHAPTER 2

The Impact of
Gang-Related Violence

An Innocent Bystander Falls Victim to Gang Violence

Harry Fletcher

In November 2007, Harry Fletcher received a call from his eldest son, who said that his best friend's brother, Etem, had been present near the scene of a gang gunfight and was fatally shot. Fletcher describes the funeral and aftermath and evokes the devastating effects Etem's death had on his family and the entire north London community where the incident took place. He bemoans the gang situation in his community and calls for governmental intervention into what he calls the "out-of-control weapon crime" present in many English cities.

On 15 November last year [2007] I received a phone call from my eldest son, saying that his best friend's brother, Etem Celebi, had been shot dead in Stoke Newington at 9.50 PM the previous evening. We both felt disbelief, grief and a sense of hopelessness. Within hours, the killing had been named the 23rd gun crime of the year in London. A statistic.

Underneath the Statistics

Underneath was a devastated family, a shattered community, and broken friends. Etem's brother Firat had gone on holiday with us and both were regular visitors at my home, watching their beloved Arsenal [an English soccer team].

Etem was 17. His parents, Kemal and Hayriye, were from northern Cyprus. Etem had attended local schools and was a student at Brooke House Sixth-Form College studying sports science. He played football [known as soccer in the U.S.] for Leyton and, in recent months, for the under-18s at Dagenham

Harry Fletcher, "Shattered Lives: Last Year, 26 People, Mostly Young Men, Were Killed in Gang-Related Shootings in London," *New Statesman*, January 21, 2008. Copyright © 2008 New Statesman, Ltd. Reproduced by permission.

and Redbridge FC [English football team]. He had been Player of the Year and Players' Player of the Year, winning trophies since the age of 11. His many aunts and uncles, nieces and nephews, lived around Famagusta [Cyprus].

Friends said of him: "He constantly made people laugh. He was bright and intelligent." His father said: "People loved me because I was his dad and loved him because he was my son."

I went with my son to visit the scene of the shooting on the Friday following the killing. We arrived at 8.30 PM. Already the community had made a makeshift shrine, with scores of bunches of flowers, football shirts and mementoes. The scene was extraordinary, a gathering of more than forty American-ised 17- to 20-year-olds, their faces showing utter disbelief and shock. I had known many of them since they were at primary school.

The next day, I visited the family. Etem's father was unable to speak, his mother was under sedation, the extended family was in bits. During the next few days, relatives flew in from Cyprus, all unable to comprehend the enormity of what they were seeing. Over the following weekend, the family asked me to act as family spokesperson and to liaise with the police. I agreed and helped prepare statements.

The Scene of the Crime

The circumstances of the killing began to emerge. A small group of friends had been returning from the Angel in Islington [a famous London inn] and were hanging around a street corner talking to a friend who was leaning out of a window. Later, according to local youths, two young men approached the group. They asked them if they lived round the estate and the boys said they did. The two newcomers then pulled out guns and fired indiscriminately. The group fled, running to houses, heard screams, and within seconds realised Etem had been shot.

His parents ran to where he had fallen and held him in their arms for the few remaining minutes of his life. Within seconds, scores of neighbours were out in the streets, phoning the police, phoning for ambulances, trying to keep Etem conscious. The police arrived within minutes, the ambulance moments later. The emergency services did what they could, but the wound was too serious and Etem died.

In the days after the killing, Etem's friends and neighbours were struggling to cope with grief, but wanted to get organised. I suggested holding a ceremony and tribute exactly one week after the murder. The young friends printed T-shirts with a picture of Etem, made badges and dog-tags. I prepared a short speech and suggested a two-minute silence. As the day approached, there was significant interest from the Turkish and Cypriot—but not the British—press. I held an impromptu press conference at the scene on the afternoon of 21 November.

The Funeral

Later, hundreds of members of the community, mainly youths, gathered at the shrine. By 9.15 PM it was pouring with rain. Despite the downpour, Etem's neighbours and friends stood in silence. I read out the statement and four or five of Etem's friends attempted to make contributions. All broke down in tears. Etem's teacher spoke, as well as a clergyman from the local church. Etem's grandfather spoke through an interpreter. Etem's mother arrived and thanked the crowd through a welter of grief and tears; and a local woman, who had lived on the estate for years, made an impassioned plea for an end to gun crime. She received moving applause.

Throughout these terrible days, the murder squad, through a family liaison officer, kept the family informed and gave full support. Arrests were made and charges followed. But the family's grief was made worse when the coroner was unable to release the body. Eventually, and thankfully, he was able to do so. A service, attended by hundreds, was held at the local mosque and Etem's body was flown to Famagusta for burial. About 20 of his friends, including my son, went to Cyprus to show solidarity with the family and support Etem's brother Firat.

I struggle to think of any thing that has affected me personally more than this killing. It was unnecessary, senseless and an appalling waste of life. The incident tore the heart out of the estate. Families have moved, and immediate relatives do not want to visit the area ever again. Since Etem's killing, two more young people have been slain by knives and guns in London. As a consequence, there are more armed police on the city's streets than before. The police can still use prevention measures such as acceptable behaviour contracts and conditional cautions with most troublesome young men but, chillingly, the number for whom enforcement (tags, curfews, incarceration) is the only response is growing. Placing further strain on overstretched police resources is the fact that increasing numbers of witnesses require protection placements.

As I write, tension between gangs in north London is described by community workers as being at the highest level anyone can remember. Some youths even wear body armour. Half a dozen gangs operate in the Borough of Hackney and scores more in the surrounding areas. The tension seems territorial, the influence of the gangs linked to postcodes. There is evidence of intimidation and involvement with drugs.

Effects of Gang Violence

Essentially, these gangs do not care about the damage they do to others. The macho culture dictates that gang members be "badder" than their opponents. Consequently, the crimes increase in seriousness, their behaviour becomes more threatening, and punishments such as tagging, antisocial behaviour orders or unacceptable behaviour contracts start to look meaningless. The levels of alienation and exclusion are extraordinary. Many feel coerced into joining gangs in order to feel protected from rival teams and from fear of victimisation if they do not.

Efforts are being made to find a lasting way of marking Etem's memory. Police, local clergy and the constituency MP [governmental representative] have held meetings. The community is planting trees and painting murals. It is possible that the youth club will open again, with structured activities that the community wants and needs. Attempts will be made to bring together all the bereaved families of gun and knife crime in Hackney.

But a political response is needed, too, not just in London, but in cities such as Liverpool, Manchester and Birmingham, where there is evidence of out-of-control weapon crime. We need to map the extent of the problem, consider the facilities available to bring young people into mainstream society rather than exclude them, and look at the relevance of education, standards of parenting and the quality of life of those involved. If macho behaviour and guns are the only ways young men feel they can gain status, the problem is certain to careen out of control.

More armed police may lead to more armed gangs and more deaths. Increasingly, we will suffer the economic consequences of violent crime. Certain areas will become unviable as places to live or do business in. If, or when, this happens, perhaps the necessary investment in excluded youths will happen. If not, we face the Americanisation of our estates and communities.

The government must act now, and visibly.

A Prison Guard Gives His Perspective

Bill Valentine

Bill Valentine spent over twenty years working as a prison guard in the state of Nevada. He has studied gang tattoos extensively as a means to help law enforcement personnel identify gang members. His book, Gang Intelligence Manual, *outlines his findings. In the following interview with his publisher, Paladin Press, Valentine talks about the gang activity he has seen in the prison system. He sees gangs, especially Mexican drug cartels, growing in power and influence. Valentine describes life as part of the prison system, relationships between prisoners and guards, and the ongoing threats of violence.*

P*aladin Press: Has the gang problem improved at all since you published your first book, or is it only getting worse?*

Bill Valentine: Sadly, the problem of illegal gangs has continued to rise. Small-town America, at one time isolated from big-city crime, has awakened to ponder the realities of graffiti, group lawlessness and drive-by shootings in their once quiet neighborhoods. This expansion of gang activity from the larger cities into rural America may be attributed in part to the efforts of big-city gang members who have relocated in order to further expand their criminal activities and empires. Despite the ever-increasing law enforcement presence, gang activity continues to be one of the nation's gravest problems.

How has the ability to identify gangsters helped police and prison guards deal with gang violence and other activity?

Gang tattoos are still the best single identifier an officer can use when validating gang membership. Using this criteria, street gang investigators are compiling volumes of identifying photos and other data on suspects. This information is stored on computer databases, disseminated and shared with other cooperating departments nationwide. This has greatly enhanced the ability of law enforcement agencies throughout the country to identify and apprehend criminals. On the street, of course, the mere wearing of a tattoo is not a crime and is only used as an identifying feature. However, inside the nation's prisons, the wearing of a gang tattoo can send the inmate to max lockup for years. In California, for instance, when an inmate is validated as a gang member, he or she is immediately given a high-risk classification and moved to a high-security institution.

Gang Activity Spreading

What is the newest challenge on the gang front—both on the street and in prison?

The newest challenge on the gang front must be the emergence of the violent Mexican drug cartels. These cartels are run by the most ruthless gangsters yet seen in the Western Hemisphere, outdistancing even the Colombian drug merchants. Just across the border in Tijuana, cartel members have slaughtered scores of police officers, judges, prosecutors, innocent bystanders, and entire families, including children. On February 27, 2000, Police Chief Alfredo de la Torre Marquez, 49, driving alone after attending Mass, was cut down by cartel members who pulled alongside his Suburban and opened fire with semiautomatic weapons. Responding police counted more than 100 bullet holes in him and the car. As of this date, no suspects have been arrested in his slaying. However, one of the cars used by the assassins was recovered and found to have been stolen in Chula Vista, California, which exemplifies the ease with which these persons move across the border. And herein lies the threat to us. Nearly every major U.S. city has reported the emergence of Mexican immigrant criminals, many of which have ties to these drug cartels.

Inside the nation's prisons, this is even more evident. Mexican immigrants—Border Brothers, Sinaloan Cowboys, and other sophisticated criminal family members—are forming their own prison gangs. These imports, at times, will cooperate with the existing gangs in controlling the prison drug markets. Others disavow this practice, preferring instead to engage in open warfare with these existing gangs for complete control of the prison rackets. And in some of our prisons, where these immigrants now outnumber the local talent, they do indeed control the drug market.

In your opinion, which gangs pose the biggest threat today and why?

Difficult to say, since they are all a threat to the nation's security. But those that come to mind first are the ones that have developed a rigid structure and maintain a strong leadership and are expanding nationwide. This includes all gangs that ride under the People Nation (Latin Kings and Vice Lords, for instance) or the Folks Nation (Gangster Disciples).

These two pervasive organizations are spreading their poison nationwide by recruiting extensively in disadvantaged areas throughout the United States. And alarmingly, they have targeted schools and playgrounds as recruitment pools. This practice of getting to the nation's impressionable youth so early may be creating a generational split that will be difficult to overturn. And to compound the problem, young females are joining the gangs and becoming every bit as violent as are their male counterparts.

Another threat, often overlooked, is the political clout these two "nations" have developed. In south Chicago, for instance voting blocks made up of thousands of youthful gang sympathizers have been able to sway the outcome of local elections. Local political hacks play on this power, in many instances, by developing strong friendships with suspected gang leaders.

Relating to Gang Members as a Prison Guard

When you were working as a prison guard, how was your relationship with gangbangers?

Working inside the walls for years afforded me the opportunity to observe gang members (and other inmates) with their façades stripped away. By this I mean a perceptive officer working face to face with these people, year in and year out, should be able to discern and use to his or her advantage the weaknesses, strengths, and other characteristics and peculiarities of prisoners—traits not so easily perceived by the street cop.

I got along fairly well with most inmate gang members. I say, most, because there were others—confrontational inmates—with whom I didn't get along at all. And as a line sergeant, I was expected to do what was required to maintain security in the prison. With this type of inmate, the taser, OC gas [pepper spray], or other use of force was generally necessary to gain compliance. I personally didn't like to spend a lot of time talking or negotiating with prison gang members. With them, I learned that talking was time consuming and usually inappropriate.

Fortunately, most of the hard-core gang members were in lockup. This was the preferred method of controlling their activities. That way, when one acted out or otherwise became a problem, the problem was isolated to a small area—usually his cell.

When out of his cell for a visit, classification, or other procedures, the lockup inmate was usually restrained by leg and belly chains. The exception to this was when the inmate was out for exercise, usually in a restricted pen and where there was overhead gun coverage. (Correctional officers do not carry firearms in prison. Gun coverage is provided by the perimeter towers and the rooftop gun posts and catwalks.)

Violence in Prison

Did you ever feel your life was threatened?

There were many times my life was threatened by unruly inmates. But conwise inmates will not threaten correctional officers because doing so brings heat down upon them. For instance, we might have torn apart a threatening inmate's cell many times in a single week while looking for weapons. Things like this disrupt a prisoner's day-to-day existence, and so most of them are not so vocal (although they may be harboring such thoughts). But to answer your question, prison correctional officers are grossly outnumbered by inmates. And if the inmates prioritize harming you above everything else, they will do it. They have the numbers, the patience, and the strength to do so. A correctional officer has to accept this fact and, of course, be prepared at all times to utilize whatever advantage he or she may have to prevent this from happening. Fear of the consequences prevents most inmates from carrying out their threats.

How did you deal with the day-to-day threat of violence, and what was your most effective tactic for avoiding it yourself?

Contrary to popular thought, violence in prison is not a daily event. Most days pass uneventful. Although there are times when prison violence is carefully conceived, most of the time it is unexpected and jumps off suddenly. I learned to discern the subtle cues that signaled impending problems. These include one or more inmates trying to stare the officer down, unusual groupings of inmates on the yard, more inmates asking for protective custody, increased canteen sales, increased hostility directed at the officers, and the time-tested "gut feelings." Another invaluable help was information gleaned from reliable informants.

Every savvy correctional officer who works the yard and is face to face with inmates develops informants. Reliable informants will let the officer know who is making weapons, who is dealing drugs, who is planning trouble, and any other significant circumstances. Does the inmate play a dangerous game being a snitch? Absolutely! Snitches and baby rapers (child molesters) are considered the lowest forms of life in prison. Many have a short life span. What do the snitchers expect in return? Favors: extra food, phone calls, a state television set or radio, a different cell mate, a prison job with a pay number (salary), or any number of other things that tend to make time a little easier. Does the officer step out of bounds by providing informants with perks not available to the rest of the population? Yes, he or she may. But it may be a matter of survival to do so.

Thoughts About the Future

Do you see any end in sight in terms of gang activity on the streets? What do you think is the best way to try to curtail it?

Drive-by shootings, mayhem, and other violent criminal activity have become a nighttime occurrence on America's streets. I see no quick end to it. I think the courts should hand down mandatory prison sentences for anyone convicted of these types of crimes, especially if a weapon is involved.

The feds could do more by mobilizing gang task forces and going after the guns of the law breakers, while lightening up on the law abiding citizen. . . .

And I personally feel the citizens should be allowed more freedom in defense of their lives, homes, and property. I support sensible gun ownership by law-abiding citizens along with concealed weapon permits. The jurisdictions where this is allowed show a sharp reduction in crime.

Victims' rights. We have all watched the courts bend over backward to ensure the guilty party is afforded all of his rights, while ignoring the plight of the victim. This is wrong and should be amended. The victim is most often the forgotten party.

Citizen patrols working under the guidance of law enforcement agencies can be a valuable tool in neighborhoods that have a high crime rate. Graffiti hot lines work to alert the police of areas frequented by gang members. In conclusion, it becomes imperative that the law-abiding citizen take an active role in identifying and reporting to the police the presence of gang activity in their neighborhoods.

A Gang Member's Funeral

Peter W. Marty

Peter W. Marty is a pastor at a Lutheran church in Davenport, Iowa. He had not had much contact with gangs until he was asked to conduct a funeral for a young gang member named Jamal, who had been killed in a gang-related shooting. In the following selection, Marty relates his experience as pastor at Jamal's funeral. Before the funeral, he was approached by two police officers, who told him they would be present to keep order and offered him a Kevlar vest for his protection. He declined the vest, but he remained behind the pulpit for the entire service. He watched as almost six hundred people filed past the casket, one of whom had probably killed Jamal. Marty concludes the selection with thoughts about how the experience changed him, and how he thought it might have affected those who attended.

When George called to ask for help with his grandson's funeral, I didn't hesitate. I'd do anything for the man. George is a gentle soul, born with an impulse for counting others first. When he's not helping his wife shuffle through her daily maze of Alzheimer's, he's at the hospital, sitting with hurting people for hours on end. I've seen his patience. When the words to match the pain aren't there, he lets the tool of his trade—a small pectoral cross on his tie—do all the talking. At the nursing home, he serves as a private translator. As the visiting pastor, I move in and about the wheelchairs with bread and cup. George whispers to me as we go: "She can do it. She needs help. He can do it." I confidently insert a taste of God into the mouths of those who cannot feed themselves, and act as if I know them as well as George does.

"This is going to be a little different funeral, Pastor," George says. "Jamal didn't have anything to do with the church. But he was a really sweet kid. He just had a habit of hanging around with the wrong crowd." At the funeral home I meet George and his daughter. If George's heart is cracked in two, the boy's mother's heart is a crumpled heap. Pam is the one who brought Jamal into the world with so much hope only 17 years earlier. The funeral director informs me that this will be a large funeral—"huge," he tells me after the family leaves.

Police Plan to Attend the Funeral

Nobody has put together an obituary yet. But the morning paper reports that Jamal was riddled with bullets from a gang-related shooting. Two men show up unannounced in my office the next morning. As if on cue they flip open I.D. badges and ask to talk with me. Henry heads up the local gang unit investigative squad. Bob is the point person for community policing in the neighborhood where Jamal was gunned down. When they give me a quick primer on gang warfare in the city, I feel unusually ignorant.

"We fully expect rival gangs to be attending tomorrow. We're here to assure you that the two of us will be working on safety inside the church. We'll have eight squad cars running extra patrols outside the church." A SWAT team will be standing by in unmarked vans at the back of the church. Revenge killing, the men add, is their greatest concern.

Henry asks if I want to wear a bulletproof vest for the service—it's standard procedure for them. "But it's up to you." I glance at the canvas bag on the floor and decide that this isn't the time to start fussing with something I don't understand. Jesus' instructions come to mind: "Take no bag, no tunic, no sandals, no purse." I'm sure he meant to include a Kevlar vest on that list. I begin to have visions of the vest bulging awkwardly beneath my white alb. "No thanks," I tell them politely.

Gang Members Pay Their Respects

Henry and Bob are back the next day in plainclothes, both of them with radios and small weaponry beneath their jackets. When the mourners began to pour in, the air grows tense. Henry eyes every guest coming through the door, and greets those he knows. When a gang leader and his bodyguards step from a car, Henry elbows me gently, "You're looking at the most dangerous man in town." I learn to spot gun holsters under pricey suits. Jamal's killer hasn't been identified yet, but Henry tips his head to indicate a young kid standing against the far wall—the leading suspect. He's also one of the pall-bearers.

For two hours, shrieking friends and silent mourners with cold, distant faces file past Jamal. They dump everything from bullets to lavish gold necklaces into the mahogany casket. I wriggle my way through the lobby crowd to check on the progress of the line. A few of the more serious wailers have collapsed on the carpet with dry heaves. The funeral director and his associates are white with fear. I'm trembling.

Nearly 600 people pack into the church. Henry has positioned himself behind the organist in the rear balcony while Bob patrols the lobby. I have predetermined two things: the service will break all records for brevity, and I will conduct the entire ceremony from behind the pulpit (as if the half-inch oak plywood provides protection from gunfire). What on earth do these worshipers in their various stages of rage want to hear from a white pastor who didn't know Jamal, and who lives his own sheltered existence? As far as I know, these street toughs want nothing to do with a church.

I feel out of place in my own church. But I have resolved to preach the gospel with everything I have to give. After all, George doesn't look as if he is feeling out of place. Why should I? He seems to take the day and the service in stride, probably because he loved his grandson so thoroughly, and loves the Lord so purely. None of the external commotion seems to bother George. If I can absorb even a fraction of the peace that resides in him, seated there in the second pew, maybe the words of the sermon will fall together.

Then the 13-minute funeral service is over. I slip out the pulpit door. Since the police have asked the family not to hold a graveside service, I am officially finished. A small fight breaks out among a few people who want the casket reopened. Henry helps clear the church. George hangs around with his daughter and a few close friends who have come to support him. We trade glances. I walk over to him and we embrace. "Pastor, you'll never know what this means to me."

Reflections on the Experience

I may never know how much this means to George. But I know what his presence and this day meant to me. They've changed me. My "pastor's" perspective in uncomfortable settings is not as "bottled up" anymore. There's more of a self-forgetfulness now—I pay less attention to peripheral things. I notice that other people set aside certain hang-ups, even potent ones like hatred and fear, when they get really thirsty for God. Like Jacob wrestling in the night with God at the Jabbok River. Someone jumps him out of nowhere and turns his fear into purpose.

I too have some fresh ways to look at fear, some new ways to size up grace. After Jamal's funeral, it began to occur to me that his friends might be more scared of the church and its potential for good than I ever was of them. I began to wonder if they weren't more nervous about what God might want to say to them than I was about their reaction to me. When Jacob fought with God, he didn't receive a clear victory. But he did discover a new capacity for reliance on God. My own fight to maintain focus on that tough day has not meant that I'm never afraid. But I feel drawn to lean more confidently on God—and to absorb some of the peace that resides in grace-filled people like George.

A Teacher's Perspective

M. Garrett Bauman

M. Garrett Bauman teaches at an inner-city community college. His students face the many challenges of inner-city life, including gang activity. Bauman himself grew up in a ghetto neighborhood but managed to escape that life to become a teacher. In this essay, written beside a pond during a school break, Bauman reflects on the difference between his life and the lives of his students. He considers that the stillness of the pond and the fact that he got out of the ghetto should help him find inner peace. But he concludes that being involved in the messiness of his students' lives is more important to him and that being with his students is where he finds peace.

In the faint predawn light, fallen leaves crunched underfoot. Our two-acre pond had shrunk to one-third its normal size in this dry season. I hiked here before sunrise to shake off the stories my students told me, stories that made me thrash at 5 A.M.

From my 74 acres of isolated woods and creeks, I would later that day commute to my community college's inner-city satellite campus in Rochester. I knew how privileged I was to have escaped the ghetto where I grew up, literally across the street from infamous Eastside High School in Paterson, N.J. I had lived amid the senseless gang wars and brutality portrayed in the film about the school, *Lean on Me*. While I now returned to my country retreat daily, there was no such escape for my students. The day before, a 30-year-old man had wept in my office, grieving over the death of his brother, shot by a rival drug dealer. Although his three brothers dealt and used

M. Garrett Bauman, "From Turmoil to Transformation," *Chronicle of Higher Education*, vol. 51, October 29, 2004, pp. B24–B25. Copyright © 2004 by *The Chronicle of Higher Education*. This article may not be published, reposted, or redistributed without express permission of the author.

heavy drugs, Jamal had been clean for a year. He wiped his eyes. "They're all going to be dead soon! This is my second brother killed." Jamal had abandoned gang life to attend college. He planned to disappear and reappear as a new person, as many community-college students do. He had sold his expensive stereo, guns, and car to finance his education. He washed his clothes in the kitchen sink, ate at soup kitchens, and feared he would not have enough money to scrape through the semester.

I also thought about Pamela, with her two chronically ill children. Her daughter with sickle-cell anemia required emergency trips to the hospital every few weeks. Her 13-year-old son had had a colostomy and wore a bag to contain his waste. A schoolyard fall or a punch to the stomach could kill him. Yet she sent him out each day because she would not allow him to disappear into institutions. "My boy's going to live as much as anybody in this world," she told me. "If he dies tomorrow, at least he's going to live first." She could have been speaking for herself. Pamela was a superb student, hungry to improve. But her hands shook and her flesh had shrunken in the struggle to obey her hard will. Earlier I had advised her to reduce her volunteer counseling of rape victims, asking her how her husband and children would manage if she became seriously ill from her frenetic pace. "But it's important!" she protested. "These women have no one. They're suicidal."

"Are you?" I asked.

That made her grin. "I've got an ulcer. I put my worry there; that way I know where it is."

Overcoming Significant Obstacles

These days, many students at all colleges deal with drugs, diseases, legal problems, abuse, and family crises that affect their capacity to learn. But there are more of them at community colleges. In one of my classes, all 21 of the women were single mothers. In another, two-thirds of the students had been formally diagnosed with attention-deficit disorder. Such realities give superficial credence to the simplistic stereotype of community-college students as third-rate. Yet many of my students, including ones in these classes, were well read, brilliant, energetic, and highly successful later in life. Many who might appear in statistical studies merely as mediocre achievers or dropouts made heroic efforts to overcome burdens that would crush students with easier lives. A "C" in academics often is the equivalent of an "A+" in life.

Violence is routine among my students. One class was talking about a shooting when I entered the room. A half-dozen had been aboard a city bus as gang gunfire erupted in the street. The bus driver, like some Gabby Hayes stagecoach hand, kicked the diesel horses into high speed and careened around a corner as my students dove to the floor, using book bags for shields. "My math textbook could stop anything," one boy said. Some laughed nervously; others clenched their jaws and stared grimly.

How can a person achieve enlightenment in such a world? Can a teacher transmit eternal truth, or even mundane truths, to people shaking in terror or exhausted with worry? I was no Buddha, no wise rabbi. I lacked the inner peace that I thought my students needed from me. My monkey mind chattered with scenarios of failure.

Seeking Peace

That was why I hiked to the pond. Teachers have often come to water to look into themselves and reflect. "Budh," the root word of the great teacher's title, means "to awaken" but also "to fathom a depth, penetrate to the bottom." I hoped to learn from the water, to disappear into it for a while and reappear renewed. Like my nearly emptied pond that filled in spring, like my students who dared to remake themselves, a teacher must be reborn each season too.

As the sun rose, the pond reflected the trees' reds and golds and the ether-blue sky. The still water captured even the flutters of leaves. I envied the pond's calm as my own mind rippled with shadowy memories of students who had disappeared from my roster. Latoya, James, Natalie, Ramon. Their ghostly faces seemed to drift beneath the water.

If only my mind, and my students' lives, could be as calm as the water I contemplated, free of life's noise and chaos. Imagine what Jamal might accomplish in school if he did not have to deal with former addicts banging on his door to demand bags of cocaine, if he did not dread having perhaps contracted HIV during his years of using needles. Imagine what Pamela might do if she were not distracted by platelet counts and emptying bags of fecal waste. Imagine what I might teach my students if their personal burdens did not distract and haunt me.

Like many professors, I've had more than my fair share of peace and quiet, with summers free to think about higher things. Publishing assignments have let me label as "work" kayaking on foggy lakes at dawn and daydreaming in a Caribbean rain forest beside a waterfall with only Arawak ghosts for company. Yet now I was as unsettled as a harried caseworker or stockbroker. I had the traditional ivory-tower life of a professor, but where was the quiet pond inside myself?

A Model of Transformation

I squatted on the hardened mud shore. On the pond bottom, leaves had settled into brown ooze to be absorbed into next year's weeds. Here was a quiet model of transformation. As I studied the pond bottom, an inch-long mayfly nymph crawled through the silt. It rolled a dead leaf into a tube around itself for winter. In spring, it would emerge, rise to the surface, and live a few glorious weeks in the air. As I peered closer, I saw dozens of leaves rolled in the silt with mayflies inside. I also spotted a dragonfly nymph hunting mayflies under water.

When it located one, it unrolled the leaf and seized the twitching mayfly around the middle with powerful jaws. The dragonfly too would grow wings and fly next spring, to hunt the surviving flies in the air.

Was it possible to see the violence of my students' lives from such a perspective? Their transformations were harried and threatened on all sides; their moment in the air might be brief; some might never fly. But they dared to complete their metamorphoses. I would remember this when Pamela phoned me from the hospital where she was writing a paper, while her moaning daughter endured an excruciating blood transfusion to treat her anemia. Instead of fretting over the unfairness of her task, I would admire her energy and determination. Her life was anything but peaceful; yet she defied the turmoil, continued to grow and transform herself. I could not tell her or Jamal that peace would come, or that a college degree would protect them from the terrors that stalked them. But I could tell them that it was possible to become more than they had been before.

I realized that the pond's stillness, like the removed life of contemplation, is largely illusion, ephemeral at best. Our intellects live inside our messy lives, not apart from them in some Platonic realm. My discomfort arose from reluctance to allow my students' noise and pain into my quiet, country life. I had wanted to continue thinking of myself as one who had escaped the ghetto. But I mistook the cure for the sickness. To seal myself inside the ivory tower of my discipline was not to be safe but perhaps most in danger, most ripe for misery as a teacher. Teachers can't be happy when they are isolated from their students' lives. But when I accepted the messy chaos of Jamal and Pamela's lives as part of their education—and part of my own—I began to find the quiet that had eluded me. This is what I have learned in my 33 years of teaching at a community college—and I have to relearn it each semester.

CHAPTER 3

Working to Curtail Gang Activity

Slowing Down Gang Recruitment

Laura Stevens

Len Untereiner is president of Spirit Keeper Youth Society, an organization in Edmonton, Alberta, Canada, that helps Aboriginal youth learn to lead healthy lifestyles and gives them alternatives to gang involvement. The term "Aboriginal" is used to describe members of a number of Native American tribes in Canada. Untereiner speaks to groups of students about gangs, attempting to diffuse the sense of glamour surrounding gangs and to give them a realistic picture of the drugs and violence that they would face as part of a gang. Untereiner was himself a gangbanger in the 1950s. In this interview with Laura Stevens of the Alberta Sweetgrass *newspaper, Untereiner talks about how gangs have changed over time and describes his work helping young people to avoid gang recruitment.*

Former gang member and now president of Spirit Keeper Youth Society (SKYS). Len Untereiner, talked to the Ben Calf Robe school students to shatter the images that glamorize the gang lifestyle.

"You need to talk to these kids when they're young and let them know that this is an illusion," said Untereiner. "I hate that word, gang, because it glamorizes, it glamorizes the lifestyle that is criminal."

Untereiner told *Sweetgrass* that he didn't want to go into details about his involvement in gangs, however he did say that the gang lifestyle today is completely different than what it was in 1950.

Laura Stevens, "Group Wants to Slow Down Gang Recruitment," *Alberta Sweetgrass*, February 2006, pp. 3–8. Reproduced by permission.

Being a Gangbanger in the 1950s

"When I was a young gangbanger in the 50s, we weren't into drugs. It was other stuff, like recruiting kids to fight turf wars," said Untereiner, a band member from Carry the Kettle reserve [reservation] in Saskatchewan.

"They don't recruit kids anymore into gangs to try and build it for toughness. The whole recruiting thing now is to sell drugs. Therefore, what I say in the workshop is gangs will use a multi-level marketing system and their product is drugs, specifically crystal methamphetamine, also known as crystal meth, crank, tweak and ice."

Why Kids Join Gangs

Untereiner said that when the average person reads about gangs, they learn about the violence, drugs and abuse, but he said what people don't look at is why kids join the gang life.

There are numerous reasons why kids might join, but growing up without a father figure, parents that are too strict, and fear seem to stand out more for Untereiner.

"A lot of kids will join a gang because they are having so much trouble at home, but they don't realize that when they get into a gang it's 10 times worse," said Untereiner. "The discipline is corporal; in other words they get beaten. Young guys are in as much or more danger of getting beaten, stabbed, or killed from their own gangs than they are from opposing gangs. Kids will join a gang out of fear, fear of reprisal."

As Untereiner spoke about the cold realities of the gang life on Jan. 27, little snickers, whispering and spiteful looks could be seen and heard from the young crowd. However, most kids seemed to be hanging on Untereiner's every word about pursuing a different and positive path.

Making a Difference by Reaching at Least One Kid

Untereiner said that if one kid understands what he's talking about during the workshop then that, "is what makes a difference because it's one less kid joining a gang."

"You talk to a hundred kids, maybe one kid will get it, but if you talk to a thousand kids maybe 10 will get it and that means 10 kids won't enter a gang," said Untereiner.

Just within Edmonton, Untereiner said, there are Lebanese, Asian, Pakistani, Black, Vietnamese and Chinese gangs in operation, however Aboriginal gangs seem to get more attention. Why?

"Well, because they're easy pickings," said Untereiner.

"Many of the Aboriginal youth that are in the city come off the reserve with no skills, no education and can't find jobs so they can be easily recruited in the Aboriginal gangs."

Gangs Mixed Racially

However, Untereiner explains that Aboriginal kids don't necessarily stay within the Aboriginal gangs. They will go where the money is greater.

"Not all Native kids work for Native gangs. If they could make a better buck working for an Asian gang, they will sell drugs for them," said Untereiner. "For example, if you ran an Amway business and tried to move the product, you wouldn't care what race, creed or color the person was doing the selling for you. This applies to the drug trade."

Sweetgrass asked Untereiner if there were any risk to himself because his organization is helping a potential drug seller or gofer out of the gang life.

Slowing Down Recruitment

"We don't get into the gang's business; all that we're trying to do is to stop young kids from joining gangs," said Untereiner. "We only focus on intervention and prevention and as long as we keep doing that, we are not hurting them. In addition, what we're doing is hardly even noticeable. However, it's noticeable to the mother whose young kid decides not to go into a gang because we talked to them."

Len Untereiner said the society has "moved and worked with kids who have had hits on them and we saved their lives. If you save one life that validates your whole organization."

Untereiner stressed that his society does not work with the police in any way, therefore kids who are involved in gangs or who are being scared into one are encouraged to go to SKYS for support and a safe place.

Gangs Will Always Exist

Untereiner said there is a mutual understanding between him and some of the gang members higher up the organizational chain.

"We don't report on gangs, therefore they let us live so they don't bother us," said Untereiner. "If we started fighting the gangs, they would put us out of business in a heartbeat and I know this because I know the gang mentality. We are not in their business, but we are in the business of slowing down the recruiting and trying to discourage kids from that particular lifestyle."

The reality is that gangs will always exist, said Untereiner. However, the SKYS group wants to make the communities stronger and keep as many kids out of gangs as possible through gang intervention workshops, counselling services, child and youth learning centres, Aboriginal awareness training and mental and social health programming. These are just some of the programs and services offered to those in need.

"We know that gangs are not going away, but we can stop or prevent kids from joining," said Untereiner. "I remember the [Edmonton] mayor saying that we are going to wipe out gangs by the year 2008. That was the most idiotic statement that anybody could make. I'm sure you could hear the gang members laughing all over Edmonton because that's never going to happen and to think that you can do that is folly. How are you going to do that? Buy a machine gun and shoot them all? It's stupidity."

A Former Gang Member Helps Girls Find Other Options

Isis Sapp-Grant, as told to Mary E. Medland

By the time she was fifteen, Isis Sapp-Grant had been arrested for assault and robbery, and her boyfriend had been murdered. She was a member of the Deceptinettes, a gang of girls in Brooklyn. Thanks to the support of a police officer and some of her teachers, she was able to turn her life around, complete high school, and go on to college. While she was in college, she worked at a detention facility for girls on Staten Island in New York. At that time, she recognized the abuse the girls had suffered in their own homes, and she saw them as victims who were acting out in the only way they knew how. The plight of these girls inspired Sapp-Grant to found the Blossom Program a number of years later. The program offers case assessment, advocacy, workshops, and a safe place for girls from twelve to eighteen, where they find supportive adults who want to help them.

I was the middle of three sisters who were raised by a single mother in Brooklyn. My high school had a lot of violence, as did the neighborhood in which we lived. When I was 15, I was a member of the Deceptinettes, a gang of girls. At this time, I really was in need of help: I had been arrested for assault and robbery, and my boyfriend had been murdered. Fortunately a police officer assigned to the gangs unit and a couple of my teachers believed in me, and I managed to cut my ties to the gang and finish high school on time.

Working at a Girls' Detention Facility

From there I went to Fisk University, in Nashville, and after two years transferred to Stony Brook University, on Long Island. I took a lot of classes in psychology and social work and ended up with a liberal-arts degree. My first job, while I was still in school, was working at New York's detention facility for girls on Staten Island, and in most of those girls I saw a reflection of myself. I remember thinking that they were smart and resilient, but that they came from homes where there had been some sort of abuse, whether sexual, physical, or emotional. These girls were victims; they were acting out and ending up in the juvenile-justice system. Worse yet, the system would see several generations of women from the same family. The cycle just kept continuing.

After I left the detention facility I went to work at the Madison Square Boys & Girls Club for four years, which eventually led me to the work I'm doing now. At the same time I worked there, I was going to New York University for a master's in social work—I knew that with that degree, I'd be taken more seriously. While at the club, I did a lot of youth-development work, helping children learn life skills, leadership development, and how to get into college. While this program worked with at-risk children, it wasn't able to deal with high-risk kids. Or if these high-risk children actually made it into the program, they would get into so much trouble that they would be forced out. I also began doing a lot of speaking engagements on my own about the needs of high-risk children at community recreation centers, churches, and so forth.

Hearing from Girls Who Needed Help

After leaving the club, I spent some time working as an administrator for the 1199 SEIU [Service Employees International Union] League Grant Corporation, a huge union that represents people who work in hospitals. At the same time, I was still hearing from girls whom I'd met in the detention facility, and I realized they needed a place that would really help them turn their lives around after they were released back in the community.

So, in 1998, after leaving 1199, I established the Youth Empowerment Mission, which allowed me to continue motivating, training, and speaking to young people and communities that were affected by violence. I'd been doing this on my own since I was in college, but now I was able to do it full time.

Much of what I did, and what we still do at YEM today, was working with families and girls who were affected by gang violence, talking to community and church groups, counseling the children, and doing training for law enforcement. The first couple of months were just a continuation of visiting organizations. I even traveled as far as Switzerland to talk to delegates of the United Nations about the correlation between racial disparities, poverty, and violence, and spoke to students in the Harvard University School of Education. I talked about how children were crying out for help but faced many obstacles, such as not even having transportation to get to social services.

But I knew that workshops and presentations weren't enough. I simply didn't see anyone working with those high-risk girls who needed case management, educational services, or help dealing with a father who couldn't keep his hands off them. These children certainly weren't Girl Scouts—they had seen too much and endured too much—but they deserved a place where they can safely define who they are, and who they were to be, in this world.

Founding the Blossom Program

In late 1999, with funding first from the New York Women's Foundation and then with grants from the Robin Hood Foundation, Sister Fund, Pinkerton Foundation, and the Independent Community Trust, we were able to rent space in an empty school that was owned by the First AME [African Methodist

Episcopal] Zion Church and establish the Blossom Program for girls from ages 12 to 18. Today I have a staff of five, and we run an after-school program that sees about 50 girls daily, and a smaller group on Saturdays. Many of them are trying to get out of the gangs they're in, and many find their way to us by themselves. In addition, we're on call seven days a week.

We knew that for this to work, the Blossom Program had to offer a single-sex environment and that when these children are here they will not have to deal with the issues that come with boys being present. In addition to doing a case assessment of, and advocating for, the children in the program, we have workshops on anger management, a group for girls who have been sexually abused, a leadership program, and a therapeutic writing workshop. If you come here, you will also see girls doing their homework or practicing yoga, taking step-dance, sewing, or cooking classes. We even have a woman who comes up from Miami every other week to teach photojournalism.

I'm always amazed at the resiliency of the girls who are part of our Blossom Program, just as I remember being amazed by the resiliency of the girls in the Staten Island facility. These children come here and their spirits are so broken that what they need is for someone to see the beauty that is in them. That's our work, and it is work that is constantly in progress. No matter how difficult these children may seem at first, the potential is there. It is *always* there, and we are just about helping these girls see that potential and believe in it themselves.

A Counselor Talks about Her Work with Gang Members

Lisa Taylor-Austin

Lisa Taylor-Austin is a counselor who has worked with gang members of all ages on both the East and West Coasts. In this essay, she discusses her feelings about gang members and their treatment by society. Taylor-Austin is neither in favor of nor opposed to gangs. As a counselor, she believes it is her role to listen and understand them. She expresses concern that young people feel they need to join gangs to have a sense of community and belonging. Although she does expect gangsters to be punished for their crimes, she believes that some of the money spent on correctional institutions could better be spent on prevention and intervention, instead of leaving these tasks to nonprofit agencies. She encourages everyone to consider their own actions before passing judgment on others, and to think about ways other than incarceration to respond to society's problems.

People often ask me why I decided on a career working in the gang world. I have been fortunate to work with East Coast gang members, West Coast gangstas, 12-year-old gang members and the most notorious of gang members serving life sentences in prison. An OG [Original Gangster] Crip in a supermax [prison] once asked me, "What is it like to sit across the table from a killer?" For me, it was an educational experience.

I am often asked if I am for (in favor) or against (opposed to) gangs. I have come to understand that it is difficult for people to understand that I am neither. This, of course, has a lot to do with my training as a psychotherapist. We are trained to be neutral and not have bias. This is the only way we can help our clients. Neutrality is the basis of our profession. Gangs exist and it is my role to seek to understand them, explain them to the public so they may understand, and, when asked, counsel gang-involved individuals who seek assistance. Other than that it is not my role to have a moral opinion about their existence.

Gang Members Are Either Glorified or Despised

Over the years I have noticed our society either glorifies gang members or despises them. The media has latched on to the gangsta lifestyle and has helped to proliferate gang life across America. Others cannot see past the label "gang member" to see that there is an individual with fears, wants, desires and hopes. Gang members are referred to as animals or often worse. It still surprises me that the persona of "gangster" can instill fear in professionals from all disciplines. We tend to fear gangs or despise them. I suppose we fear that which we do not understand. Psychologists say we despise that which is a reflection of a part of ourselves we do not like (think on that one!).

Some people tell me that if I was the victim of gang crime I would feel differently about gang members. Well, I have been the victim of gang crime. Once my apartment was robbed by an 18th Street gang member who had been released from prison less than 24 hours earlier. Another time I was in the middle of a gang retaliation shooting and watched as three of my students were gunned down in front of me. A third time I was in the middle of a shoot-out between police and Crips while I was on my way to get lunch and stopped my car at a red light. Did it have an effect on me? Absolutely. In the end it only motivated me to want to learn more, to help more, to intercede where I was invited (one cannot work with gang members unless you are invited into their life and world). Being a victim of gang crime has not made me hate gang members. It has only enabled me to see that there is a greater need for work in the gang area. The gang problem is not a police matter. It is a community matter. We all have a stake in it. What does it say about us as a nation that our children feel the need to join gangs to have a sense of belonging, community, feelings of success and feelings of power? The gang issue belongs to all of us, whether we choose to accept that or not. Why are we so quick to label people and cast them out of society? What does that say about us?

No, I am not for or against gangs or gang members. Gangs exist. Gang members exist. Maybe we should just start dealing with that instead of passing judgment.

For some reading this it will be interpreted that I believe gangsters should not go to jail or serve time for their crimes. If you are thinking that, where did you get that notion from? There are consequences for behavior in society. We all pay the price of our decisions. For some that price is paid in jail. For others we pay the price in different ways.

Advocating for Intervention and Prevention

Nearly a quarter of a million youth are in custody in public and private juvenile correctional facilities in the United States. Approximately 10 million children have a parent who has been imprisoned or under criminal justice supervision at some point in their lives. If we can spend billions of dollars building supermax prisons to house gang members, why can't we spend billions of dollars on intervention and prevention? Why are non-profit agencies the ones to bear the burden of this endeavor? Do we really want to do something about the gang problem or do we just want to lock 'em up and throw away the key? Think hard before you answer that. Chances are, with gangs growing the way they are, you either know a gang member, have a friend whose child is a gang member, or live near a gang member. If we keep incarcerating people, soon half the US population will be locked away in jail. What is the cost on America? Let's come up with new inroads and responses to our country's issues.

Before we pass judgment on others, I believe it is important to first look at ourselves. Have we done that? Are we willing to do that?

I have to say that Father Greg Boyle (Homeboy Industries) put it best, "We stand by those on the margin hoping one day the margin will change." After all aren't we all people of this planet? We have more in common than we even realize.

Tookie Williams Speaks from Death Row

Stanley Tookie Williams, interviewed by Amy Goodman

After spending over twenty years on death row, Stanley Tookie Williams, one of the founders of the Crips gang, was executed by the State of California on December 13, 2005. The following selection is taken from a telephone interview that took place two weeks before the execution. In the interview, Williams talked about how his attitude changed during his time in prison, leading him to devote much of his time to sending the message to children and youth to stay out of gangs. He also shared his thoughts about the death penalty, and his feelings as the time of execution approached.

Amy Goodman: *Stanley Williams, can you describe where we're talking to you right now?*

Stanley Tookie Williams: Well, I am on San Quentin's death row. I'm in a cell that's probably nine by four or nine by five feet. . . . And there's a steel sink. There's a steel toilet. There's a steel bunk. There's a steel shelf. There's a light fixture. And on the bars is—on the outside of the bars is a mesh fence.

You have been at San Quentin for more than half your life?

Yes. Yes. Unfortunately so. Quite pathetic.

Can you talk about your time there? Can you talk about the beginning, the years in solitary confinement and what you've done?

Well, I can quite—I can easily demythologize the thought that, well, a person, when he goes to prison, of course, they'll change. They're locked up. That's not so, because I was incorrigible from the moment I got here all the way up to 1988, so

Stanley Tookie Williams, interviewed by Amy Goodman, "A Conversation with Death Row Prisoner Stanley Tookie Williams from his San Quentin Cell," *Democracy Now!*, November 30, 2005. www.democracynow.org. Reproduced by permission.

that debunks that theory. And once I was in solitary confinement, it provided me with the isolated moments to reflect on my past and to dwell upon something greater, something better than involving myself in thuggery and criminality. It had to be more to life than that. It had to be more than the madness that was disseminating throughout this entire prison.

Starting to Change

And so, when do you feel like you started to change?

Between the years of 1988 to 1994, and it's a continuous—it's an incessant reality for me. My redemptive transition began in solitary confinement, and unlike other people who express their experiences of an epiphany or a *satori* [awakening], I never experienced anything of that ilk. Mine—that wouldn't have been enough. I often tell people that I didn't have a 360-degree turnaround; I had a 720-degree turnaround. It took me twice as much. Just one spin around wouldn't have done it. I was that messed up, that lost, that . . . brainwashed. So, I was able to gradually in a piecemeal fashion change my life slowly but surely through education, through edification, through spiritual cultivation, battling my demons. And eventually, that led to me embracing redemption.

And what does embracing redemption mean? Can you talk about your writing? Can you talk about what you have done?

Well, my interpretation of redemption, it differs from the theological or the academical rendition. I believe that my redemption symbolizes the end of a bad beginning and a new start. It goes beyond, in a sense of being liberated from one's sins or atonement in itself. I feel that my redemption mostly or primarily encompasses the ability to reach out to others. I call it—when people say spirituality, I break it down as a spirit act, with "spirit" being the [essence] of the soul, the id, etc., etc., and the "quality" aspect of it being an act, a performance, a deed. So, we're talking about a spirit act, a spirit act towards helping other people, which are primarily youths in my case.

Sending a Message to Youth

And what is the message that you are trying to send? Who are you talking to among the youth in this country?

I'm talking to any youth who are considered to be or deemed to be at-risk or even hinting around being a thug or a criminal of any type of genre. I mostly propagate education and the need for it, because to me, that is the terra firma on which any human being must stand in order to survive in this country or to survive anywhere in the world, in dealing, you know, with every aspect of civilization, every aspect of surviving. Education is very important. It took me all of these years to discern that, and now I do.

Stanley Williams, can you talk about why you started the Crips?

Well, I mean, I stated it in my memoir, *Blue Rage, Black Redemption*, that we started out—at least my intent was to, in a sense, address all of the so-called neighboring gangs in the area and to put, in a sense—I thought I can cleanse the neighborhood of all these, you know, marauding gangs. But I was totally wrong. And eventually, we morphed into the monster we were addressing.

In what way?

Well, we became a gang. We became exactly what I had odium [hatred] for, which were gangs, street gangs. I mean, there were—they became a pest. They were a pest. Every time I looked up, my friends were being preyed upon. And when I came from camp, I decided to create something that would deal with them, to put them in their place. I mean, it's—it's really ironic, because we did too good of a job, and we morphed into what we were fighting, what we were battling against.

Stanley Williams, your critics say you might be running the Crips from death row. What is your response to that?

Well, I say that whomever says that, whatever institution or singular person says that, that you must take that and society must take that with a grain of salt. I say that, because of the simple fact that I have documentation in which—if you know my editors of the books, of my children's books, Ms. Barbara Becnel, she can forward you or email you the chronicles that I received from the Institutional Classification Committee that commended me on my positive program over the last ten years, and that's dated on August 5, 2004. So, that in a sense contradicts anything that anyone is saying. This— what they're saying, these lies, these spurious allegations that these people are throwing out there are just something that they're putting out there in order to exacerbate, to expedite my execution. I mean, any time that they can make it appear as though I'm still a monster, then society will say, "Well, kill him." It facilitates my death. Common sense. That's what it does. That's what these people have been trying to do for the last five years with impetus. This is what they have been doing.

Proud That He Has Changed

Stanley Williams, what are you most proud of in your life?

Other than writing the children's books and my memoir, my redemption and my change. I never thought, ever, that I would be able to change because of the simple fact [that] thuggery was all I knew. I lived it. I breathed it. Being a Crip was all I knew. I thought there was nothing else. I dreaded life after Cripping. I dreaded that. But I say to any individual who is in a gang that if you have enough courage to get into a gang, you should have equally enough or even more to get out of it.

What message do you want people in this country to hear right now? And the governor, if you were meeting with him yourself?

Well, once again, I must say that I am innocent, and I understand that it's difficult for a person who is poor, a person who has a criminous background, as I have, a person who is black, a person who is minority. It is very, very difficult for an individual to obtain justice, as I have seen. It's very difficult. And I feel that justice should not be predicated on a person's creed or color or race or social strata or intellectual prowess or any of that. . . .

Facing the Death Penalty

Where did you get the nickname Tookie?

That is not a nickname. That is my middle name. My mother gave me that. In fact, that was my father's middle name, as well. And I believe it's my grandfather's middle name. But I know it's my father's, for a fact. Stanley Tookie Williams III.

December 13 [2005, the scheduled date of Williams's execution] is just two weeks away from this conversation.

Yes, it is.

What are your thoughts facing your death?

I have none. In other words, I continue to live my life day by day, or shall I say, minute by minute, hour by hour, and day by day, as I have been doing since my redemption. It has nothing to do with a cavalier attitude. It has nothing to do with machismo or manhood or some pseudo code of the streets, which I formerly used. It has to do with my faith in God and my redemption. That's why I can sit here and talk to you just as calmly or any of the other journalists who have crossed my path. I don't fear this type of stuff. I'm at peace. . . . And when you maintain this sense of peace and you live by truth, by integrity, these things don't bother me. It doesn't. I have been experiencing moribund type experiences most of my life. I could have died many a times. I could have died when I was shot. I could have died when I was shot at by the police and rival gang members. There were many opportunities for me to die. Of course, I don't want to die. I mean, after my redemption I have what I consider to be a joie de vivre, so, you know, I have an enjoyment, a love for life. So that's why I can calmly sit here and speak to you or anyone else with peace in my heart and peace in my mind. I don't get rattled. Nothing can rattle me. Nothing will ever rattle me. I have been rattled the majority of my life.

Regrets Creating the Crips

I asked you what you are most proud of in your life. What do you most regret?

Creating the Crips. That is my—I rue that more than anything.

You managed to strike a peace accord. How did you maneuver that between the Crips and the Bloods?

Well, the fact that a person such as me, of my ilk, who deemed the opposing gang as an eternal enemy, it wasn't hard for people to believe me, because they knew where I stood. There were no clandestine or latent messages. Everybody knew where I stood. And for me to come out and say that what we were doing was wrong, it was believable. That's why people didn't—or at least the gang members didn't discredit my propensity and my alacrity for peace. That's why I was embraced with sincerity by those who I knew and those I didn't know on both sides of the fence.

Stanley Williams, what does it mean to have the level of support that you have right now?

It's God-inspiring to me, awe-inspiring. It's excellent. I'm exceptionally grateful. I never expected it. The majority of my life, I have fought, especially in here, alone. Even—I even had to fight against the attorneys, the incompetent attorneys, appeal attorneys, appellate attorneys, rather, that I had representing me, who were not qualified. I had one attorney who was an employment litigator, job litigator, you know, on the federal level, and she had been on that for like three years, and this woman was coming to represent me for four murders?

Then they had a guy that represented me. He only represented me for six months, because after that, he had to end up leaving and going to Ireland somewhere. Now, he knew prior to that that he had an engagement, but yet he took the case, allowing me to think that he was going to be permanent. He said he was going to be permanent. But yet, still, he left within six months. As a matter of fact, it was five-and-a-half months in which he left.

So, these are the things—these are the type of representations that I was getting, attorneys who would file a brief, a 27-page or 45-page brief with over 120 typos in it, and telling me that, "Oh, well, you know, the judge wouldn't—it doesn't matter. They won't look at that." Of course, they'll look at that. And they'll use that against me, not her, me.

Thoughts on the Death Penalty

What are your thoughts on the death penalty, in general?

The death penalty, it's not a system of justice, it is a system of—a so-called system of justice that perpetuates a, shall I say, a vindictive type of response, a vigilante type of aura upon it. We're talking about something that is barbaric. We're talking about something that—it doesn't deter anything. I mean, if it did, then it wouldn't be so many—especially in California, we're talking about over 650 individuals on death row. And if it was a deterrent, this place wouldn't be filled like this. And it's an expensive ordeal that—the money, as you know, the monetary means comes out of the taxpayers' pocket.

And for anyone to think that murder can be resolved by murdering, it's ridiculous. I mean, we look at all of the wars that we have throughout other countries and other nations, and all it does is—this violence, all it does is engender violence. There seems to be no end, but a continuous cycle, an incessant process of blood and gore that doesn't end. And through violence, you can't possibly obtain peace. You can, in a sense, occupy a belief of peace; in other words, through this mechanism of violence, you—it appears that because there is a standing army or standing police that is used in brutality or violence or a system that uses brutality or violence that that is going to totally eliminate or stop criminous behavior or criminous minds or killings or what have you, but it doesn't. There has to be another way.

Do you ever imagine yourself being free?

In my dreams. In my dreams I've envisioned my liberation many a times. As a matter of fact, I was telling an individual the other day that in my dreams, whenever I run into some albatross or some type of dilemma, I seem to float away from it. And in my mind, that is a sense of freedom. That is a sense of avoiding, eschewing or shunning any type of madness.

Do you know how the state plans to kill you?

Well, if I don't, I'd have to be living in a cave somewhere.

How will they do it?

Well, through, you know, the intravenous use of needles and things of that nature.

Are they preparing you for this now?. . .

Well, yes. I'm in a different area. I used to be in East block, and now I'm in North 6. So, yes, yes, they are, of course. In their minds, it's a done deal.

And in your mind?

I'm sure they're looking forward to it, because they have come out propagating that I should be executed. Isn't that amazing? This is unprecedented for the C.D.C. [California Department of Corrections] or San Quentin prison—and/or San Quentin prison to come out against an individual; it's never been done before in the history of this institution, or the history of C.D.C. But yet, they have come out.

Can you explain what you mean?

Well, I mean, they have—you find there are individuals they have, like for instance, the San Quentin spokesperson, he spoke out. He said—even on *60 Minutes*, they did a program about me, and he stated that I deserved to be executed. Now, I believe that's taking your job too far. And at one time, they had a lot of spurious allegations on the C.D.C. website, which they had to take off, because the former San Quentin warden, Vasquez, he stated that San Quentin appears to be trying to promote death by getting into this. They're supposed to be impartial. Their job is only to execute me, not to exacerbate by drumming up the need, the protests, or the remonstration for me to be executed, but that's what they have been doing. I'm the only human being that's ever been on death row that they have ever put forth effort to execute. . . .

Thoughts on the Possibility of Clemency

If the Governor, if Governor [Arnold] Schwarzenegger, grants you executive clemency, what will you do? What are your plans? What do you want to do?

There's so many things. I'm glad—excellent question. I'm glad you asked that. The thing is, recently, I had a visit with Bruce Gordon. He is the President and C.E.O. of the NAACP [National Association for the Advancement of Colored People]. I had a visit with him on the 25th, Friday, and we have established a partnership to create a violence prevention curriculum for at-risk youth throughout America, and each of the chapters of NAACP are implementing this program. And he is going around the country promoting this and apprising people. So I'm not sitting back on my laurels, believe me.

I have things to do. I have books that I haven't even completed that I'm still working on. As a matter of fact, I'm working on *Thoughts of Thunder*. It's a compilation of essays on a variety of topics. I'm working on a female gang [book] that's called *Female Gangs: The Forgotten Gender*, and a few other books. I'm doing some other children's books, as well. So, believe me, I would be working on this, and my attorneys, you know, will be helping me strive to inevitably prove my innocence.

Do you think you could be granted a new trial?

Well, that's dealing in hypotheticals, and I don't deal with hypotheticals. I can only say that I pray that I get a new trial. I pray that I get whatever is necessary to spare my life, so that I can continue to strive in order to prove my innocence.

And if you still spent the rest of your life in jail, do you think it would be worth being spared the death penalty?

Oh, well, of course. I mean, where there's life, there's the ability to continuously strive to do whatever your purpose is or goal is in life. So, yes, if I'm alive, I can always strive forward to prove my innocence, regardless of how long it takes, even up to the last second of my life, and I'm 100 or whatever. You know what I mean? . . . As I stated earlier in the conversation, that I have joie de vivre. So with this love of life, I have it. I assume that was forged down to me from my ancestors. . . .

Last Words

Well, in these last seconds that we have, they're yours. What do you have to say?

Well, I want to thank you for allowing me to be able to express my thoughts and feelings, and that as long as I have breath, I will continue to do what I can to proliferate a positive message throughout this country and abroad to youths everywhere, of all colors or gender and geographical area, and I will continue to do what I can to help. I want to be a part of the—you know, the solution.

A Church Community Offers an Alternative to Gangs

Romulo Emiliani, interviewed by National Catholic Reporter

Romulo Emiliani is a Roman Catholic bishop in the diocese of San Pedro Sula, in Honduras. When he arrived in Honduras from his native Panama, he became aware of the problems of gangs from his experiences preaching in the jails. He got to know and understand gang members and has spent much of his time working with them, including acting as a mediator in a conflict between two powerful gangs. Emiliani is sometimes referred to as the "gang priest." In this interview with National Catholic Reporter, *Emiliani talks about his work with the gangs and his belief that the church's response to these young people should be love and compassion instead of fear and disgust.*

NCR [National Catholic Reporter]: *You came to Honduras in order to serve as the auxiliary bishop in San Pedro Sula. You were going to lead spiritual retreats throughout the country, but you quickly made news because of your public contact with youth gangs. Some even call you the "gang priest" or the "Bishop Salvatrucha" (after the name of one of two prominent gangs). How did you get involved with the gangs?*

Romulo Emiliani: I knew I was coming to a country with big problems of poverty, family disintegration and all types of violence, but I really didn't know much about the gangs. Shortly after arriving I began to feel there was a grave problem for these young men in the gangs. They were killing each other. Since I preached in the jails, it was there that I entered into contact with them and began to understand their world.

It's a very special world, very complex. I began to understand them and I began to love them as well. When you know someone well you can't help but love them in the situation they find themselves, as difficult as it may be.

I kept getting closer to them. And then I offered myself as a mediator in the big conflict between the Calle 18 and the Salvatrucha [the two largest—and most antagonistic—gangs]. I started to work with leaders of the two gangs, but I wasn't aware at the time of what this was going to involve. At times the Holy Spirit demands a lot of you and complicates your life.

I started a foundation that's going to build a big rehabilitation center for youth from the gangs. Today I'm in touch with them a lot and I understand their world. All of them are the fruit of a serious problem of poverty, of lack of education, of hunger and family disintegration. We've got to help them.

It seems that many of these young men join the gangs because no one else—including the church—is organizing them or offering them alternatives. What lessons can the church learn from your experience with these young people?

They have a great sense of belonging, of cohesion, and they have a lot to teach us about what it means to live in community. Unfortunately, theirs is a world of delinquency. But they have a great sense of belonging. That's why they mark themselves with tattoos that can never be erased. They feel committed to their gang. It's the group that has become their family, and they love the group to the extent that they're willing to give their life for it. That's a lesson for Christians. Yet, lamentably, the gang members commit crimes, consume drugs, and lead lives that are very sad.

If the church is going to respond better to them and their violent environment, what does the church have to do? What type of ministry does the church have to develop in order to respond to this urban scene?

First the church has to understand that part of its mission is to search for, attend to, and accept those whom no one loves, giving signs of what the love of God can do. See them with compassionate eyes, and look for ways to open spaces in the parishes for them. Not to see them with disgust, nor with fear. It's a big challenge for the church to help rehabilitate the gang members. They are the lost sheep, as the parable says, and the good shepherd leaves behind the 99 others to go look for the one that's lost.

An Ex-Prisoner Becomes a Gang Specialist for the Police

Pernell Brown

While serving time in prison, Pernell Brown was active in gang activities and violence until he joined the Nation of Islam. This group helped him learn about his own self-worth and taught him to be proud of his African heritage. Brown was released from prison after seven years, and he now works with the Portland, Oregon, police department as a gang specialist. He helps the school district in education planning for at-risk youth and works with individuals and groups of adolescent African American and Latino males. Brown was once a member of the Bloods gang, and now is proud to work side by side with a former member of a rival gang, the Crips. Together, the two men show youth how to choose friends by their character, not what gang or "set" they belong to.

My name is Pernell Brown, and I am currently a Gang Specialist with the Community of Colors Program of the North East Coalition of Neighborhoods in Portland, Oregon.

I was from the 6800 Block Woodlawn Park Bloods. I went to prison in Oregon for assault with a deadly weapon. In 1989, I received a 10-year sentence with a 5-year mandatory minimum, and I served 7 years.

While in prison, during the early years of my sentence, I continued my "street" mentality. I sold drugs and continued "banging." I did not work on schooling. I worked on my criminality. The atmosphere is that you will be a part of something and that you survive. Survival was the name of the game.

Pernell Brown, "Statement to the Commission on Safety and Abuse in America's Prisons," *Commission on Safety and Abuse in America's Prisons.* www.prisoncommission.org/statements/brown_pernell.pdf. Reproduced by permission of the author.

I was highly respected, because I not only had older brothers in jail banging, but also because of the person I was. I was quick to fight. I never ran my mouth. As I got comfortable in the prison system, I learned the "two for one game." I learned how to sell drugs inside of the walls. I learned who to get down with and who not to touch. I would work on "finances" with the shot callers in the white and Hispanic gangs.

Violence in Prison

Prison was a breeding ground for my violence and me. New folks coming to prison claiming sets [gangs] but who had not been initiated were prime targets. Gang fights or a drug deal gone badly were reasons to exhibit violence, and I took advantage. There were those that would pay for protection from gangs.

Criminals have twenty-four hours per day, seven days a week to develop and engage in criminal scheming. "Criminal pride" or "respect" are major contributors to fights and other violence. Having to be at the top of the food chain means you do what you have to do to maintain your status and that your peers accept you.

Logistics or territories play major roles in violence. I must be able to move my products and people to make money and maintain my safety. Race plays a role in the violence. I had an altercation with a member of a white supremacy gang and have a scar above my left eye, and he bears the disfigurement for a lifetime of shattered jawbone.

Prison made me bitter, not better. The staff did not treat me with dignity or respect. Even now, when I go to work inside of some of the prisons, corrections staff will say inappropriate comments as if I am still an inmate. I have to remain professional and set them straight. The mentality or belief that "once an inmate always an inmate" is alive and well inside the institutions' staff. Nor did the staff model what pro-social behavior looked like. The Department of Corrections staff was as crooked as those of us that were locked up.

I did not see any pay value in quitting the gang, and the prison did not offer me any alternatives early on in my incarceration. The administration started cutting programs soon after I got into prison—there were no vocational courses, no college courses, even weights (for weight lifting) were limited. Programs were available only for those who had more or less time in their prison sentence than I. "We're not paying for your education—you're not worth it" was the attitude.

Joining the Nation of Islam Changed His Life

After serving three and a half years, I joined the Nation of Islam. Joining opened up a completely new world for me. I felt as though I had removed blinders from my eyes. I began to understand my self-worth. I came to know that I came from African Civilizations, African Kings and Queens. I came to realize my responsibility to my community and myself. I was made aware of the sacrifice and struggles that others had been through in order for me to have a better life if I so chose. I was able to see the destruction I had caused to myself and to people in my community. I learned that "the white man" was not killing our people—gang members were. We were killing each other.

Working as a Gang Specialist

Now I am a Gang Specialist and I am a Certified Alcohol and Drug Counselor. I am an alumnus of the African American Program of the Multnomah County Department of Community Justice and continue to support graduates of the program upon their re-entry to the community from prison.

In my role as a gang specialist, I am involved in case planning and case management of adolescent African American and Latino males. I work closely with educators of the Portland School District to develop alternative education planning for at-risk students. I am a part of a crisis response team. I respond to community incidents and am on site for all community events. I attend all school sports events that are determined to have a high propensity for gang violence. I facilitate support groups in the public school classrooms and in the community. I advocate for both adjudicated and non-adjudicated clients in the courts and Department of Child Services. I am involved in mentoring young African American men, educating them in their rich histories.

I work as a voice for clients advocating justice and develop recommendations with the Portland Police around issues of injustice in the African American community. I work with an ex-Crips gang member. He and I have a great relationship. I am actually proud to say he is a very good friend. When my co-worker, Carl, and I facilitate groups with gang members, and they hear our histories of being from rival gangs, they often respond to us with questions about how we "get along" when we are from opposite "sets." This is very effective in opening up a dialogue with these young cats. We are able to stimulate them to ask questions. I feel grateful when I am able to leave them with healthy messages and lessons. I am very fortunate to have Carl as my co-worker and friend. From this I have learned that a man becomes my friend or associate by his merits, not his "set."

A Family Man

I am the father of four children. I have two sons and two stepdaughters. I am the grandfather of two boys and five girls. My oldest son graduated from the University of Oregon with a Bachelor's degree. He is currently attending the University of New Mexico. He is in the draft for the International Soccer League. My youngest son is currently attending Concordia University and is playing basketball and maintaining a 3.5 grade point average. I have a good relationship with my youngest stepdaughter, who is a professional in the Atlanta, Georgia, area. My oldest stepdaughter and I are working on our relationship continuously. I am proudly parenting five of my seven grandchildren. I am involved with all aspects of their lives. I am giving them the sense of love, nurturing, belonging, and family identity that will break the cycle of violence in my family. I teach my children and grandchildren on a daily basis their responsibilities for themselves. I talk to them about being proactive in their own lives. Most importantly, I model the behavior for them.

Organizations to Contact

The editors have compiled the following list of organizations concerned with the issues debated in this book. The descriptions are derived from materials provided by the organizations. All have publications or information available for interested readers. The list was compiled on the date of publication of the present volume; the information provided here may change. Be aware that many organizations take several weeks or longer to respond to inquiries, so allow as much time as possible.

American Civil Liberties Union (ACLU)
125 Broad Street, 18th Floor, New York, NY   10004
(212) 607-3300 • Fax: (212) 607-3318
e-mail: aclu@aclu.org
Web site: www.aclu.org

The ACLU is a national organization that works to defend Americans' civil liberties as guaranteed by the U.S. Constitution. It opposes curfew laws for juveniles and others and seeks to protect the public-assembly rights of gang members or people associated with gangs. The ACLU publishes the biannual newsletter *Civil Liberties*.

America's Promise Alliance
1110 Vermont Avenue, NW, Washington, DC   20005
(202) 657-0600 • Fax: (202) 657-0601
e-mail: joinalliance@americaspromise.org
Web site: www.americaspromise.org

America's Promise Alliance is committed to seeing that children experience the fundamental resources they need to succeed at home, in school, and out in the community. These fundamental resources are described as the "Five Promises" (caring adults, safe places, a healthy start, an effective education and opportunities to help others). Together with its local and regional partners, the organization sponsors a number of initiatives and National Action Strategies to achieve its goals. *America's Promise Bulletin*, a weekly newsletter, and other publications are available on the Web site.

Boys and Girls Clubs of America
1275 Peachtree Street, NE, Atlanta, GA   30309
(404) 487-5700
e-mail: info@bgca.org
Web site: www.bgca.org

Boys and Girls Clubs of America supports juvenile gang prevention programs in its individual clubs throughout the United States. The organization's Targeted Outreach delinquency prevention program relies on referrals from schools, courts, law enforcement, and youth service agencies to recruit at-risk youths into ongoing club programs and activities. The organization publishes a quarterly newsletter, *Connections*, which can be accessed through the Web site.

Campaign for Youth
e-mail: campaignforyouth@clasp.org
Web site: www.campaignforyouth.org

The Campaign for Youth is an alliance of organizations that are concerned about the challenges confronting more than five million young people in the United States who are disconnected from education, employment, and opportunity. Established in 2002 by the leadership of national youth serving organizations, the Campaign for Youth's mission is to build a united voice for disadvantaged and disconnected youth, and to build a constituency for action.

Fight Crime: Invest in Kids
1212 New York Ave. NW, Suite 300, Washington, DC   20005
(202) 776-0027
e-mail: tturner@fightcrime.org
Web site: www.fightcrime.org

Fight Crime: Invest in Kids is a national, bipartisan, nonprofit anti-crime organization of more than 3,000 police chiefs, sheriffs, prosecutors, other law enforcement leaders, and violence survivors. The organization studies crime prevention strategies, informs the public and policymakers about those findings, and urges investment in programs proven effective by research. Programs supported include high quality early education programs, prevention of child abuse and neglect, after-school programs for children and teens, and interventions to get troubled kids back on track. Surveys and presentations are available on the Web site, as well as news releases from across the nation.

Join Together
715 Albany Street, 580-3rd Floor, Boston, MA   02118
(617) 437-1500 • Fax: (617) 437-9394
e-mail: info@jointogether.org
Web site: www.jointogether.org

Join Together, a project of the Boston University School of Public Health, is an organization that provides information, strategic planning assistance, and leadership development for community-based efforts to advance effective alcohol and drug policy, prevention, and treatment, and to address community problems associated with alcohol and drugs. Reports on a variety of key issues are available on the Web site.

Milton S. Eisenhower Foundation
1875 Connecticut Avenue, NW, Suite 410
Washington, DC   20009
(202) 234-8104 • Fax: (202) 234-8484
e-mail: info@eisenhowerfoundation.org
Web site: www.eisenhowerfoundation.org

The Milton S. Eisenhower Foundation is dedicated to reducing crime in inner-city neighborhoods through community programs. The organization identifies, funds, evaluates, builds the capacities of, and replicates multiple solution ventures for the inner city, the truly disadvantaged, children, youth, and families. Through national policy reports, the Foundation communicates what works to citizens, media, and decision makers. It also runs a strategic communications school for nonprofit organization staff and youth to help change political will and create action. Official, extensive reports on a variety of topics are available on the foundation's Web site.

National Alliance of Gang Investigators' Associations (NAGIA)
P.O. Box 608628, Orlando, Florida 32860-8628
(321) 388-8694
e-mail: RustyKeeble@fgia.com
Web site: www.nagia.org

The National Alliance of Gang Investigators' Associations (NAGIA) is a cooperative organization composed of representatives from regional gang investigator associations across the country, as well as federal agencies and other organizations involved in gang-related matters. The NAGIA advocates the standardization of anti-gang training, establishment of uniform gang definitions, assistance for communities with emerging gang problems, and input to policymakers and program administrators. NAGIA also maintains an online library of articles written by gang specialists on a variety of gang-related topics.

National Council on Crime and Delinquency (NCCD)
1970 Broadway, Suite 500, Oakland, CA 94612
(510) 208-0500 • Fax: (510) 208-0511
e-mail: aboldon@mw.nccd-crc.org
Web site: www.nccd-crc.org

The National Council on Crime and Delinquency, founded in 1907, is a nonprofit organization that promotes effective, humane, fair, and economically sound solutions to family, community, and justice problems. NCCD conducts research, promotes reform initiatives, and seeks to work with individuals, public and private organizations, and the media to prevent and reduce crime and delinquency. Two of its areas of focus are youth violence and juvenile justice. NCCD's Web site offers numerous publications on these and other crime-related topics.

National Crime Prevention Council (NCPC)
2345 Crystal Drive, Suite 500, Arlington, VA   22202-4801
(202) 466-6272 • Fax: (202) 296-1356
Web site: www.ncpc.org

NCPC provides training and technical assistance to groups
and individuals interested in crime prevention. It advocates
job training and recreation programs as means to reduce
youth crime and violence. The organization's Teens, Crime,
and the Community (TCC) initiative has motivated more
than one million young people to create safer schools and
neighborhoods. TCC's Community Works program helps teens
understand how crime affects them and their families, friends,
and communities, and it involves them in crime prevention
projects to help make their communities safer and more vital.
The NCPC publishes books, brochures, kits, posters, and reports, and many are available for downloading from the Web
site.

National Criminal Justice Reference Service (NCJRS)
P.O. Box 6000, Rockville, MD   20849-6000
(800) 851-3420 • Fax: (301) 519-5212
Web site: www.ncjrs.gov

The National Criminal Justice Reference Service is a federally
funded resource offering justice and substance abuse information to support research, policy, and program development
worldwide. The organization's Web site includes various resources and statistics about gangs.

National Institute of Justice (NIJ)
810 Seventh Street, NW, Washington, DC   20531
(202) 307-2942 • Fax: (202) 307-6394
Web site: www.ojp.usdoj.gov/nij

NIJ is the research, development, and evaluation agency of the
U.S. Department of Justice and is dedicated to researching
crime control and justice issues. NIJ provides objective, independent, evidence-based knowledge and tools to meet the

challenges of crime and justice, particularly at the state and local levels. It sponsors research efforts through grants and contracts that are carried out by universities, private institutions, and state and local agencies. A large collection of NIJ publications and NIJ-funded publications can be found on the Web site.

National School Safety Center (NSSC)
141 Duesenberg Drive, Suite 11, Westlake Village, CA   91362
(805) 373-9977 • Fax: (805) 373-9277
e-mail: info@nssc1.org
Web site: www.nssc1.org

The National School Safety Center works to promote safety on college and university campuses. It develops training tools, strategies, and materials specific to the culture and safety needs of institutions of higher learning. It publishes the booklet *Gangs in Schools: Breaking Up Is Hard to Do*, the *School Safety Update* newsletter, and other books, videos, and papers on school safety topics.

National Youth Employment Coalition (NYEC)
1836 Jefferson Place, NW, Washington, DC   20036
(202) 659-1064 • Fax: (202) 659-0399
e-mail: nyec@nyec.org
Web site: www.nyec.org

The National Youth Employment Coalition (NYEC) is a membership network that improves the effectiveness of organizations that seek to help youth become productive citizens. Toward this end, the NYEC sets and promotes quality standards; tracks, crafts and influences policy; provides and supports professional development; and builds the capacity of organizations and programs.

**Office of Juvenile Justice and Delinquency
Prevention (OJJDP)**
810 Seventh Street, NW, Washington, DC   20531
(202) 307-5911 • Fax: (202) 307-2093

e-mail: askjj@ojp.usdoj.gov
Web site: http://ojjdp.ncjrs.org

As the primary federal agency charged with monitoring and improving the juvenile justice system, the OJJDP develops and funds programs on juvenile justice. Among its goals are the prevention and control of illegal drug use and serious crime by juveniles. Through its Juvenile Justice Clearinghouse, the OJJDP distributes the annual *Youth Gang Survey* and various fact sheets and reports. The office also sponsors the National Youth Gang Center (NYGC) and several Faith-Based and Community Initiatives (FBCI) focused on at-risk youth and gang prevention.

Teens Against Gang Violence (TAGV)
2 Moody Street, Dorchester, MA   02124
(617) 282-9659 • Fax: (617) 282-9659
e-mail: teensagv@aol.com
Web site: http://tagv.org

Teens Against Gang Violence (TAGV) is a volunteer, community-based, teen peer leadership program. Its mission is to empower youth leaders by providing them with culturally appropriate knowledge, skills, tools, and relationships so they can educate others about nonviolence through peace and justice. TAGV distinguishes between gangs that are nonviolent and those that participate in violence. Through presentations and workshops, the organization educates teens, parents, schools, and community groups on violence, guns, and drug prevention.

Youth Crime Watch of America (YCWA)
9200 S. Dadeland Boulevard, Suite 417, Miami, FL   33156
(305) 670-2409 • Fax: (305) 670-3805
e-mail: ycwa@ycwa.org
Web site: www.ycwa.org

Youth Crime Watch of America (YCWA) is a nonprofit organization that assists students in developing youth-led programs, including crime and drug prevention programs, in communities and schools throughout the United States. Member-students at the elementary and secondary level help raise others' awareness concerning alcohol and drug abuse, crime, gangs, guns, and the importance of staying in school. Strategies include organizing student assemblies and patrols, conducting workshops, and challenging students to become personally involved in preventing crime and violence.

YouthBuild USA
58 Day Street, Somerville, MA   02144
(617) 623-9900 • Fax: (617) 623-4331
e-mail: info@youthbuild.org
Web site: www.youthbuild.org

YouthBuild USA is an organization that seeks to unleash the intelligence and positive energy of low-income youth to re-build their communities and their lives. YouthBuild is a comprehensive program that integrates school, work, social action, leadership development, and personal transformation. In this unique program, unemployed youth create tangible community assets such as housing, community centers, reforested land, and play areas while preparing for employment, studying to complete secondary school, learning to be leaders in their communities, and getting support to make positive change. There are now more than 225 YouthBuild programs nationwide. Annual reports and brochures can be found on the Web site, and a searchable database connects visitors to other YouthBuild publications.

For Further Research

Books

Richard Arthur with Edsel L. Erickson, *Gangs and Schools.* Holmes Beach, FL: Learning Publications, 2000.

S. Beth Atkin, *Voices from the Streets: Young Former Gang Members Tell Their Stories.* Boston, MA: Little, Brown & Co., 1996.

Michael K. Carlie, *Into the Abyss: A Personal Journey into the World of Street Gangs.* Springfield, MO: M. Carlie, 2002.

Sean Donahue, ed., *Gangs: Stories of Life and Death from the Streets.* New York, NY: Thunder's Mouth Press, 2002.

Robert J. Franzese, Herbert C. Covey, and Scott Menard, *Youth Gangs.* Springfield, IL: Charles C. Thomas, 2006.

Arnold P. Goldstein and Donald W. Kodluboy, *Gangs in Schools: Signs, Symbols, and Solutions.* Champaign, IL: Research Press, 1998.

Tom Hayden, *Street Wars: Gangs and the Future of Violence.* New York, NY: New Press, 2004.

Duane A. Leet, George E. Rush and Anthony M. Smith, *Gangs, Graffiti, and Violence: A Realistic Guide to the Scope and Nature of Gangs in America.* Incline Village, NV: Copperhouse Pub. Co., 2000.

Jody Miller, *One of the Guys: Girls, Gangs, and Gender.* New York, NY: Oxford University Press, 2001.

Marie "Keta" Miranda, *Homegirls in the Public Sphere.* Austin, TX: University of Texas Press, 2003.

Randall G. Shelden, Sharon K. Tracy and William B. Brown, *Youth Gangs in American Society.* Belmont, CA: Thomson/Wadsworth, 2004.

Evan Stark, *Everything You Need to Know about Street Gangs*. New York, NY: Rosen, 2000.

Periodicals

Michael Blanding, "Growing Up in Gangland." *Boston Magazine*, January, 2004, pp. 86–98.

U.S. News & World Report, "Dispelling the Myths about Gangs." January 21, 2008, p. 14.

Instructor, "The Freedom Writers." November–December 2004, p. 27.

Lauren Todd Pappa, "Gangs: Keep Out! Three Teens Tell Why Gangs Are on the Rise and What You Can Do to Stay Safe." *Junior Scholastic*, November 26, 2007, p. 6.

Matthew Quirk, "How to Grow a Gang." *The Atlantic Monthly*, May 2008, p. 24.

Rupa Shenoy, "The Warriors: Hardened by Gang Life, Many Young Latinos Leaving Prison Are Now Using Their Toughness to Help Others." *The Chicago Reporter*, March, 2005, pp. 15–16.

Alexandra Shimo, "In the Line of Fire: Of the Hundreds of People Who Are Shot in Toronto Every Year, the Vast Majority Live to Talk about It. They're Gang Members, Friends of Gang Members and Innocent Bystanders. Five Survivors Tell Their Stories." *Toronto Life*, January, 2006, pp. 46–52.

Benjamin Wallace-Wells, "Underground Authority: A Gonzo Sociologist Discovers How Drug Gangs Give Ghetto Life a Fragile Kind of Order." *Washington Monthly*, April 2008, p. 43.

Kai Wright, "Where Murder Won't Go Quietly: A New Kind of Gang Is Making Northeast Brooklyn the Deadliest Place in the City." *New York*, January 14, 2008, pp. 22–23.

Index